We're Not Blended—
We're Pureed

A Survivor's Guide to Blended Families

DIANA LESIRE BRANDMEYER
AND MARTY C. LINTVEDT

DEDICATIONS

FROM DIANA

For Ed—you're amazing, and I'm so thankful God put you in my *life*!

Andy, Ben, and Josh—my boys! Thank you, God, for blessing me with them.

Sara and Brianna, my daughters-in-law—how grateful I am to have you in my life. I am no longer outnumbered! God has blessed me beyond my expectations.

FROM MARTY

For Vern—you still make me laugh and bring the joy of Christ every day.

Erik and Susan, Heidi, Travis and Kristen—you are proof of God's love and immeasurable grace. I am blessed.

Published by Concordia Publishing House

3558 S. Jefferson Ave., St. Louis, MO 63118-3968

1-800-325-3040 • www.cph.org

Text © 2011 Diana Lesire Brandmeyer and Marty C. Lintvedt

Cover © 2011 CPH/Ed Koehler

Manufactured in the United States of America

Library of Congress Cataloging-in-Publication Data

Brandmeyer, Diana Lesire.

We're not blended, we're pureed : a survivor's guide to blended families / Diana Lesire Brandmeyer and Marty C. Lintvedt.

p. cm.

ISBN 978-0-7586-1791-0

1. Stepfamilies. 2. Families. I. Lintvedt, Marty C. II. Title.

HQ759.92.B725 2011

646.7'8--dc22

2011005882

1 2 3 4 5 6 7 8 9 10   20 19 18 17 16 15 14 13 12 11

In Genesis, we see God create life from nothing. In the Gospels, we see God create life from death. I often wonder which of those two is the greater miracle. Whether a blended family originates out of bereavement or divorce, either way it is formed, by the grace of God, out of some type of death. That, brothers and sisters, is a miracle that we do not sufficiently appreciate.

—Eric R. Stancliff, Public Services Librarian,
Concordia Seminary, St. Louis, Missouri

Contents

PREFACE

Be encouraged. That's what I would say to you if you were sitting across from me. There is hope as long as God is at the center of your marriage and your family. Know that there will be trying times, and there will be times of unimaginable joy. Most of all, know that you are normal, and so is your family. Don't let anyone suggest otherwise. Every family struggles with the relationships between parents and children at some point. While the struggle is often difficult and unpleasant, some of the most important work we have as parents is allowing children to learn and to grow into independent men and women. Be encouraged!

Hugs, Diana

This is Diana's story. The path that she and her husband, Ed, have traveled on their blended family journey may be similar to yours in some ways but very different in other ways. It is our hope and prayer that this book will help you see the "normal" in what are sometimes difficult circumstances, receive practical help, and be equipped with useful resources. The first part of each chapter Diana takes us into her world. Perhaps you will see yourself and your family on some of the pages. The second part of each chapter I respond using my clinical background, my mental health training, and at times my own personal history. Our goal is to provide practical suggestions and resources to help you with the difficulties, the opportunities, and the transitions your family faces.

It is our desire, Diana's and mine, that as you read the pages of this book, your real family will be blessed, and you will be encouraged.

In His love, Marty

Acknowledgments

Writing this book was not the effort of just two people. Many people stood by us and walked with us through this exciting journey.

First, we must acknowledge God's guiding hand from the beginning to the last period.

Next, we want to thank Tamela Hancock Murray, our agent, for hand-holding and praying us through this book; Scot Kinnaman, for being a fantastic editor; and CPH, for taking a chance on two crazy authors.

We extend our gratitude to Jennifer Tiszai, Jennifer Carry, and Eric Stancliff for their generous gift of time to be our first readers.

And we would like to offer a hug and thank you to those who took the time to fill out our survey.

We are blessed with patient husbands willing to sacrifice a home-cooked meal for take-out and the odd ability to live in a dirty house while this was being written. By the time you get to the last page, you will realize we don't have perfect children. But for us we have perfect, God-given sons, daughters, and daughters-in-law; and we thank Him for the joy He has brought us.

And our mothers, Audrey Ritter and Darlene Gronseth Olson! Both of our mothers have shown us what living daily by faith means, and our families and we have been blessed by your example.

INTRODUCTION

Recipe for a Blended Family

Toss in blender: One widowed mom with two sons. Add one widowed man with one son. Blend for 20 seconds until right consistency.

Hit the wrong button, and this family is past blended, we're pureed!

Can two families learn to cohabitate? In peace? Ever?

It's here! The day you've been planning for has arrived. The sun is shining, the birds are singing, and you know those kids will look adorable in those tuxedos. Life is about to become wonderful again. A two-parent household, just the right amount of children, and a new home; all that joy is waiting for you, and all you need to do is smile and say, "I do."

But then . . .

The clues were right there in our wedding album. I should have run. His son, Andy, had made a face in every one of our photos, but the clincher was the snapshot of him holding the knife as if he were going to stab the wedding cake. A substitute for me? Maybe.

That's only the beginning of my story, but I can't dwell on it. So many life lessons waited ahead for me: Changes I didn't anticipate. Arguments I could never imagine lurked behind the driver's seat in the mini-van. An "I love you, Mom" when I didn't expect it. Through it all, God never left my side.

Maybe you picked up this book because you are terrified you have turned into a version of a fairy-tale wicked stepparent.

In public, do you pretend your family is a vision of Main Street America in 1950, yet at home the battle lines are etched in the cement driveway?

Don't be dismayed. Just as God is with me, He is with you too.

"For the LORD your God is a merciful God. He will not leave you or destroy you or forget the covenant with your fathers that He swore to them." (Deuteronomy 4:31)

I'm at the end of my journey now, and I'm waiting for grandkids to arrive. I cherish Proverbs 17:6: "Grandchildren are the crown of the aged, and the glory of children is their fathers."

When disappointments loom and expectations fall short, my prayer is that you will hold this verse or your favorite Scripture in your heart. I pray that you will laugh along with me as I tell you about my own experiences. By seeing what I, and others, have learned on our journeys, you can avoid stepping on land mines as you travel down the rough brick road of stepparenting and shatter the image of the wicked stepparent. You aren't alone. Find out how others have made the switch from two families to one.

Proverbs 17:22 reminds us that "A joyful heart is good medicine." So why not make yourself a cup of tea or cocoa, sit back with this book and be merry—or just lock the bathroom door, slink into the bathtub, and answer the door only if someone is bleeding, choking, or throwing up.

1

Are the Wedding Bell Blues Becoming Your Song?

I was getting married—again! This time would be different, for now there were children involved. My boys were getting a new father; Ed's son would be getting a new mom, me. We tried to include the children in the wedding preparations, but there wasn't much about weddings that intrigued small boys.

We planned a reception for our friends and family. We hired a DJ, who sent us a playlist. Ed and I went through it, eliminating any song with the potential to propel us into our past. We let the boys pick a few songs. We made standing direction that requests from the guests were not allowed to be played unless Ed and I approved them. Our reception was to reflect our new beginning.

APRIL

Check every little detail before you walk down the aisle.

Max and I carefully planned our wedding details, making sure none of our old lives would be a part of our ceremony.

I'm divorced. The disintegration of that marriage began when I found a letter addressed to "Dear Suzie" with the lyrics of a popular love song handwritten by my ex.

Max's teenage daughter wanted to sing one song during the ceremony as a gift to us. We liked the idea but wanted to know what the song would be. She said it had to be a surprise. We wouldn't let her sing unless we knew. She refused to come to the wedding. Later we found out I would have been walking down the aisle to the same song my ex had so lovingly written to another woman. I believe God intervened and saved me from horrific memories on my wedding day.

When the boxes of invitations arrived, we encouraged our boys to stick on stamps and lick envelopes with us. Our invitations read: "Andy, Ben, and Josh invite you to witness the marriage of their parents." Notice those names are in alphabetical order!

The wedding day arrived warm and sunny. We had a quick rehearsal before the ceremony, then separated to get dressed for photos, deciding to take them before the boys managed to look like boys instead of models. Ed wanted to take all the boys with him to get dressed. With great patience he buttoned, tucked, and tied until they were ready. Except for Josh, who refused to wear the shoes. Ed ultimately convinced him to put them on by telling him those shiny shoes would make him dance faster.

At the back of the church, I waited to walk down the aisle to start a new life. In my mind glowed visions of my new family. There would be family dinners—everyone sharing thoughts about their day, discussing the book we're reading together every night before bedtime. Maybe I would even homeschool, further building the bonds between us. I couldn't be more positive that happiness would follow us all the days of our lives.

Still, what was that ugly bubble of doubt hanging over my

head? Why did I have that feeling that I was doing something wrong? And what about the hollow corner in my heart?

A year and twelve days had passed since my husband, John, had died. I had stood in this same church and silently vowed to be like Ruth, never forsaking my mother-in-law. And now I felt as if I were doing just that. Peeking around the corner, I saw her sitting in the front row next to my sister-in-law. The absence of the father-in-law I had called Dad for the past nine years sliced like a paper cut. He hadn't come, and neither had my brothers-in-law. They disapproved of this marriage. Too fast, too soon, they thought.

My two tuxedo-clad sons jiggled with excitement. I straightened their jackets and gave them a quick kiss on the forehead. "Go, it's time. Don't run." I held my breath as they walked away from me, relaxing as Josh reached the end of the aisle and took a seat next to my aunt. Just like we'd rehearsed.

My turn. My best friend had loaned me her husband to walk me out of my old life and into my new one. I threaded my arm through his.

"Ready to expand your family?" he whispered.

"Yes." I took a few steps and then realized I was almost running to the altar where Ed, his son, and my future waited. And the aisle wasn't that long!

After the ceremony, Ed and I drove away from the church holding hands. I felt like we had done the right thing. I knew the road ahead wouldn't really be as easy as I hoped. I read the statistics and knew the odds of a blended family making it, and they weren't reassuring. Swallowing the lump in my throat, I made a new vow: This family would not become a negative statistic. No matter what happened, we would stay together and work through any hardships that might come our way.

Ed pointed through the windshield at the evening sky. "Look, we've only had clear skies, no rain, but there's a double rainbow." I watched as it grew longer and higher as we drove to the reception. I thanked God for a reminder of all of His promises, for His love, and His provision. I knew then this family would make it with God's help. I held fast to God's promise in Micah 2:12: "I will set them together like sheep in a fold, like a flock in its pasture." I didn't know how smelly a sheep pen could get when it held three boys.

Getting Down the Aisle

Any wedding based on God's principles should be celebrated with friends and family, and more so if you're getting remarried. Your support comes from them, and you're going to need it! Invite them to witness your vows to each other.

Friends, more than family, may be your biggest supporters for a while. Gail, my best friend, and Fran, my sister-in-law, listened to me for hours, walking me through the logistics of moving my household, remarrying, and discovering God's purpose for me in my new life. They asked tough questions such as, "Will he attend the Lutheran church with you? What are you going to do with your money? Can you give as much attention to Andy as you do Ben and Josh?"

My friends made me think before getting married and moving from Missouri to Illinois. I would be leaving the strong support system I had built in the last year. However, though I was physically moving away, my friends were still there for me after the wedding excitement dissipated and the reality of being a blended family smacked me in the face, destroying my Norman Rockwell dreams.

LISA

Lisa wanted to bond with Jeff's daughter, and she knew mall shopping would be one of the best ways to win a preteen's heart. "I asked Kim to be my maid-of-honor instead of my best friend. I guess I hoped that would let her know I wanted our relationship to be special—like woman to woman. She was reluctant until I told her she could pick out any dress she liked. I would have promised anything to get her excited about our wedding. I quickly learned twelve-year-olds have a different definition of *classy*. The sequined dress with the feathered collar she wanted didn't qualify. After many tears, we finally found one that we could both live with."

What I didn't notice was the way Andy inserted himself between his father and me. I dismissed the way he went from independent while with me to totally dependent on his dad the minute he arrived. I ignored the building frustration, thinking once we were a family things would change.

We should have taken the crew on a weekend trip to a family counselor's office instead of the water park.

"For behold, the winter is past; the rain is over and gone."
(Song of Solomon 2:11)

Ed and Diana rested in the comfort of God's promises. They were happy, optimistic, and eagerly looking forward to the road the family would travel in the years to come. The pre-wedding warning signs didn't quite make it into Ed and Diana's peripheral vision. Many couples get so caught up in the excitement of planning a wedding and future that they miss things occurring right in front of them.

Was Andy's behavior one of those warning signs? Children frequently are barometers for a home's emotional climate. A child's ability to communicate his or her "barometer reading" is dependent on several things. Human development comes into play. It is easy to recognize the difference in ability with regard to physical change and maturation. Those who study human development often break it into three categories: physical, cognitive, and psychosocial. Just as our physical bodies develop and change over time, our cognitive abilities and mental processes evolve, and our emotional selves and personalities grow and change.

Family rules, spoken or unspoken, also impact how a child might reflect the climate in his or her home. Parents can help their kids develop an emotional vocabulary and ability to communicate feelings by first looking inward. We need to ask ourselves:

- How did I know when my parents were angry, sad, happy, or anxious? How do *my* kids know what I am thinking or feeling?

- Do I speak with my words, my behaviors, or a combination of the two? Do I communicate through silence?

- Is my method of communication healthy for me and those whom I love?

- Is the content of my communication healthy and appropriate for family members, especially children? Parents must be vigilant to protect their children from information that should be "adults only," or between spouses.

Andy, at age 7, was not a skilled communicator. Mental health professionals recognize that significant trauma can negatively impact emotional formation. Andy's emotional development may, in fact, have been arrested by the trauma of his mother's illness and death. Yet he was communicating through his behavior. Andy inserted himself between his dad and Dad's new wife. Was he trying to separate Ed and Diana or become a link between the two? Most parents assume that actions like Andy's indicate an unspoken desire to "divide and conquer." But a therapist might investigate the possibility that Andy was, through his behavior, trying to connect the pieces of two families that had become splintered, broken in fact, by death. Andy's pre-wedding behaviors may have been his way of expressing concerns he couldn't cognitively identify or verbally express but troubled him nonetheless.

Preparing for Marriage

For those readers who have not yet married, consider carefully the fact that most couples, both first-time brides and grooms and those remarrying, commit much time, money, and effort to wedding preparations and honeymoon plans. How much of your resources are committed to preparation for a lifelong marriage? Committing yourselves to several sessions of premarital counseling can help you look directly at the strengths and blessings you and your partner bring to marriage. Pastoral counseling is also a safe place in which to explore points of conflict, differences, challenges, and weaknesses. Several meetings with your pastor will enable you to check the foundation of faith upon which your marriage will be built. Praying with your pastor, reviewing the consistency of your shared beliefs or the differences that may be problematic, is critical.

Preparing for the Wedding

Once you and your intended have made the decision to marry, the next big step is determining how to tell your children. What factors do you weigh in determining the best way to carry this out? Children's ages, relationship to the future stepparent, and personality characteristics are a few things to consider. Some parents choose to gather their children together and tell them as a group. Others prefer to spend time with each child individually. Most experts suggest that sharing the news of your marriage as a couple establishes this important family unit from the beginning.

Recognizing your children's temperaments when you determine how and when to have this discussion will be important for the success of your talk.

Planning

- Putting the children's names on the wedding invitations gives them the feeling of belonging. It begins the blending process.

- Include children in some of the pre-wedding parties and showers. Giving them jobs to do, such as helping welcome guests, makes kids feel a part of the festivities.

- Dress them for the ceremony as members of the wedding party.

- Acknowledge children during the ceremony: give each child a rose or plaque with a promise of love from the stepparent to the respective new-to-them child.

LUANNE: WITH THIS RING

A circle is a symbol of unity, eternity, and completeness. The wedding ring represents eternal love and the persistently renewed promises of a couple. Some Scandinavian women wear three bands: one each for engagement, wedding, and motherhood.

In medieval England, a bridegroom would slide the ring partway up his bride's thumb, index, and middle finger, saying "In the name of Father, and the Son, and the Holy Spirit" as he slid the ring up each finger. He then placed the ring on the next available finger, the third finger of the left hand. Today, the wedding ring is an easily identifiable indication of marital commitment. Luanne and her husband-to-be had special matching gold bands made for all members of their blended family. The family members exchanged the rings during the couple's wedding ceremony.

Preparing for Change

Change can be a scary thing for adults and kids alike. How have you prepared yourselves and your children for the changes ahead?

We often forget that kids' fears may mirror those of their parents. Frequently we believe we have been successful in sheltering our children from the emotions we are experiencing, especially fear and anxiety. Think again. It's okay to remind our children that while we are excited about the new family structure we are planning, anxiety and fear are normal and to be expected.

Parents can equip their children with skills that will help manage fear. Knowledge is key. God has built an "alarm" system into our human form, a fear response that is incredible when it operates at the proper time and in the proper way. During times of danger, our fear response triggers a series of physical reactions that prepares us to act. Those physical reactions may include an increased heart rate, quicker breathing, or a churning stomach, to name a few. These physiological responses prepare us for fight or flight.

Sometimes our alarm goes off when we are not in danger. There may or may not be a threat present. When we worry, the fight-or-flight response is fully engaged to danger, whether the danger is real or perceived. It is interesting to note that the body responds the same way whether the fear is a real physical or emotional threat or an unrealistic concern that has spun out of control.

At some point in our lives most of us will experience anxiety, fear, or panic. For many individuals, change, such as blending families, is one of the things that result in very high levels of anxiety. During times of high anxiety, it is important to stop and breathe! Not quick, short, shallow breaths, but deep, slow breaths in through the nose, down to the diaphragm, and exhaled through the mouth. Slow, deep breathing lowers the pulse rate and decreases the tension felt in the body. As we relax, it is important to assess the situation:

- Pinpoint the origin of the anxious thought or fear.

- Determine if the anxiety is realistic or unrealistic.

- Interrupt unrealistic anxieties or thoughts by challenging the thought or feelings with facts.

- Problem-solve ways, including healthy self-care, to manage the circumstances. You are a steward of the gift of your body, mind, and soul. Adequate rest and proper physical, emotional, and spiritual nourishment are important components of proper self-care.

- Pray. God is listening. Studies indicate that the act of prayer and meditation effectively lowers anxiety.

As we guide our kids through the changes our families face, we teach them how to care well for themselves first by the model we set. The most important way we equip our families to manage anxiety and face fears is by modeling our confidence in God. Remember that God, our Father, neither slumbers nor sleeps (Psalm 121:3)—so we can! He will guide the process of knitting together a "whole" family from broken pieces, and His strength and faithfulness are constant.

> "Rejoice in the Lord always; again I will say, Rejoice . . .
> Do not be anxious about anything, but in everything
> by prayer and supplication with thanksgiving let your
> requests be made known to God. And the peace of God,
> which surpasses all understanding, will guard your hearts
> and your minds in Christ Jesus." (Philippians 4:4, 6–7)

2

Honeymoons Aren't Just for Couples Anymore

Before the wedding, Ed and I discussed the possibility of taking the children with us on the honeymoon. Although our main desire was to blend our family, we wanted to have the chance to bond as a newly married couple. We decided it would be better to do our honeymoon in two distinct parts. Yet it didn't seem fair to have the boys figure out how to start that process without our guidance. So, the children would stay with friends and family, while Ed and I would head out for a short three-day honeymoon.

Ed and I decided on Las Vegas because the travel packages were reasonable. We explored Hoover Dam, marveling at the sturdy structure, which seemed much like God's hand holding back evil. The desert in June baked us as we traversed the trails at Red Rocks. Some of the trails had large rocks to climb or skinny places to squeeze through. Ed helped me over the hard places, and I wondered at God's grace and His gift of this amazing man for my husband. We relished the time together—free of children.

So while we were away on our honeymoon Andy went to Ed's best friend's home, a place he often stayed and was comfortable.

Ben and Josh went to their grandparents' home in Missouri. While they were there, Ben, with his grandfather's help, made a clay pot. They baked it in the kiln for Ben to give to his new dad.

After a few slow-paced days of hand-holding and eye-gazing, we flew back to St. Louis to pick up the kids and continue with the second part of the honeymoon. Ed dropped me off at my house in Missouri, leaving me to pack my van for the second half of our honeymoon. John's mother brought my kids home. They had been bathed, fed, and dressed for vacation. She had washed their clothes, too, eliminating one giant step I had thought I would need to do before leaving. My van was packed with favorite toys and snacks. My kids were buckled in their seats. I gave my two cats one more "love you" stroke and promised them the neighbor would be over to feed them. I locked the back door, took a breath, and readied to merge our families.

We were going to spend a week in Estes Park, Colorado. The kids and I had never seen the mountains or experienced snow in the summer. Everyone was excited and ready to go.

Things did not go quite as well for the Illinois side of our new family. Ed was still making plans and doing laundry, so we didn't leave until after five in the evening. I thought we would stop at a hotel. Wrong. We drove all night and into the next day. The kids and I were pretty cranky by then. Josh had been in a car seat for hours, and Andy was learning quickly how to become a big brother and antagonize the youngest. It was family bonding at its best.

Did we make a mistake heading out west to strengthen our bonds? The jury was still out on that. I think it was a noble idea. It would have worked in the movies. However, in this real life, there were hidden issues that we had to continually confront, like a dead fish washed up on a bank. In both cases, they ended up being a smelly mess.

We rented a two-bedroom cabin, assuming the boys could stay in one room. We didn't think about the differences in our children's personalities or the established bedtimes one parent had and the other didn't. Andy is a night owl; Ben and Josh are morning people. I'm not sure why we thought they would meld into something in-between if they were bunking together. Ben and Josh complained about not being able to sleep because Andy wouldn't settle down. Andy fussed about having to turn out the lights so early.

Sometime during the night Andy would creep into our bed. Ed would return him to the room with his new brothers, come back to bed, fall asleep, and a few minutes later Andy would be back. Now, I realize he wasn't secure in this new family situation, but at the time I wasn't very understanding. I wanted sleep!

The next morning we found a mini-amusement park with go-carts and bumper boats. Josh and I watched from the fence as Ed and the other boys went around and around the go-cart track. When the time was up, Ed wanted to take Josh on the bumper boats with him. He had talked to the manager and had permission, even though the sign clearly stated Josh was too short! Ed pried him out of my fingers, promising everything would be fine. It was only Ed and the other two boys on the boats. Josh's excitement and laughter didn't sooth my worry about his safety. I applied my happy wife smile, hoping my face would soon grow numb from the pain, and took pictures. Was it too soon to have our first fight? Shouldn't we at least be back at home before lines were drawn?

That afternoon we took a sightseeing trip to the city of Boulder. That was when I discovered Ed could completely tune out the vicious barbs and finger pokes in the back of the van. Unable to endure another second, Evil Mom erupted from a place I didn't know existed inside of me. "Shut up!" I screamed loud enough to cause my throat to hurt for days. The strangers in the back quieted, and my new husband looked at me, horrified.

The differences in our parenting styles continued to be demonstrated throughout that adventure. My kids were given children's menus, and Andy ordered the most expensive meal from the adult menu. The sign on the hot tub said, "No children under 12." Andy was the only child in the frothy bubbles. While climbing trails, Ben and Josh were within arm's reach at all times, while Ed allowed Andy to climb walls and run much farther ahead than I was comfortable with. I thought this was because Andy hadn't had a mom to tell him "no" for two years. Not a problem I couldn't fix. All I had to do was get his father on board, teach him to discipline the way I did. Once we returned to Ed's home in Illinois, life would be structured, perfect even.

The honeymoon was over in so many ways. On our way back, we drove by my home to check on the cats and pick up a few things. I walked into my clean kitchen. It felt so serene, and I wanted to stay. In this house I had control, and now I wasn't so sure anyone had control. I didn't want to go back to Illinois to live with a man who never stopped driving and had apparently developed selective deafness. Had I made a huge mistake?

"But I trust in You, O LORD; I say, 'You are my God.' My times are in Your hand." (Psalm 31:14–15)

Whether or not to plan a honeymoon, the timing of the honeymoon, and selecting who will go are complicated choices each couple must decide. Many factors come into play as bride and groom determine what their best choice may be. Financial impact and availability of vacation time are among the easiest factors to reconcile. The willingness of suitable caregivers may help a couple determine if they will even have a honeymoon that includes time alone away from children.

Some couples, like Ed and Diana, choose to follow a traditional approach, honeymooning immediately following the wedding. Ed and Diana wisely opted to leave the two sets of children in the care of familiar folk and in well-known surroundings. The "blending" process was not facilitated in the absence of parents under the supervision of caregivers but kicked into high gear as Ed and Diana and the three boys traveled to Colorado together. Other couples might choose the traditional honeymoon occurring on the heels of the wedding and begin the process of settling in at home upon their return. A family vacation may be considered later, when schedules permit and some level of adjustment has been achieved.

Some couples choose to take a family trip but delay departure until after the family has had some time at home together. There is generally a hope that family routines will have become established, and the kids will be more comfortable with some of the new aspects of their blended family. While some couples will take that delayed honeymoon alone, others, like Ray and Marianne, make it a family event. After spending some time situating the family in their home, this couple and the five children they shared embarked on what they refer to as their "family-moon." Ray, Marianne, and all five children celebrated the new family unit on a camping trip, a first for Marianne and her three children. They not only survived this brave endeavor, but the family has thrived and grown to include two more children in the years since Ray and Marianne's wedding.

Appropriate and realistic expectations have a direct correlation to the success of any trip. Nothing is perfect this side of heaven! Diana spoke about the differences in Ben, Andy, and Josh's personalities, the way she and Ed had parented, and even the boys' sleep habits. Differences are not necessarily good or bad, right or wrong, but negotiating our differences typically requires adjustment, compromise, and communication with family members. As you plan for a family trip, include discussions about the similarities and differences between your children, your parenting styles, and your daily household routines. Family rules, discipline, boundaries regarding space and property, bedtimes, and study expectations are among the items you might address before you pack those suitcases and unpack the wedding gifts.

MARY

Mary and her husband took a weekend without their four shared children immediately following their April wedding. Then, in June, they loaded up the station wagon and traveled from Indiana to Arizona. Mary wrote that it was quite a trip! The family of six, plus suitcases for all, plus a cooler, made for cozy travels. "We stayed with family along the way, in motels, ate fast food, and in restaurants, and from the cooler. On our return we crossed Death Valley, then stopped for gas. We were all a little testy," said Mary. "The station owner asked us how we enjoyed crossing the desert in 125 degree heat without air conditioning. No wonder we were testy!" The next day the family made it into Colorado and threw snowballs at one another while wearing their summer shorts. Mary reported that her family enjoyed the West so much that they moved to Phoenix a year later.

Whether or not you and your intended opt to have a honeymoon, a family-moon, or stay put and begin the adjustment process in your home, taking time on a regular basis to nurture the marriage is vital. That means finding time that you and your spouse can be alone. Setting that precedent at the outset helps establish the couple as the second tier of the family's foundation, after Christ, and is important for family health.

"Pursue love." (1 Corinthians 14:1)

3

Home Sweet Home—
Where Is It?

Two homes filled with memories: mine in Missouri was a unique limestone house built in the 1800s, while Ed's house in Illinois would be a perfect size to raise a family. But which one would we choose? The obvious choice had to be Ed's home. Each boy would have a bedroom, and the house was near the business Ed owned and ran. It would have been difficult to drive from my house in Missouri to Illinois every day. However, Ed assured me he could do that if I couldn't choose to leave my home. Knowing his schedule often had him working late, and then adding an hour-and-fifteen-minute drive each way, didn't seem to leave us much choice—not if I wanted a real marriage and help with parenting.

We considered keeping my house for the weekends. With its five acres to explore and the huge stone barn where the boys could make hay forts or hang from the cow milking stations, it would make a fun getaway. Ed could use the barn to store some of his landscape supplies. We could go to my church on Sundays. There were so many reasons.

Then it was time to pay the mortgage, and we knew it wasn't realistic to keep two homes. There weren't enough hours in a weekend to maintain them both. Cutting the grass at my home took several hours, and there was a lot of maintenance to be done to the house and outer buildings. So we called a realtor and the "For Sale" sign was pounded into the front yard. I boxed up the kitchen, my books, and my decorations, and found a home for my washer and dryer.

Moving day arrived. Ed used the forklift to get my bedroom furniture from the second floor. I climbed onto the two-foot wide dormer windowsill and clutched my knees into my chest while I looked out over the back pasture and St. John's Gildehaus Church, hiding my tears. I would be leaving a home where I spent many hours stripping wood floors and trim and unearthing covered treasures. The bedroom, with a balcony off the French doors, had been finished exactly the way I had imagined. It seemed one more dream had to die before I could move on with my new life. I would be leaving a place where I had known extraordinary love and happiness. It made me sad and mad at God. And then, of course, I did the unwise thing: instead of taking my anger to God, I took it to Ed.

All of my boxes and furniture were piled into Ed's garage. For weeks I would come home from the grocery store or from taking the kids to the park and see my things neglected, stacked boxes begging to be unpacked. I would blink back the tears and hurry past them. There wasn't any room in the house for my things, maybe not even for me.

Just off our bathroom is a delightful dressing table. I longed to make it mine, but Debbi's things were still there. To me it felt like a shrine to Ed's former wife, not to be messed with. I tried to ignore the dressing table when I would get my clothes out of the closet or when I passed by to take a shower. All of my makeup and hair products I kept in the boys' bathroom. At least there I didn't feel as if I were displacing someone who was much loved.

I kept my clothes in boxes in the closet instead of the dresser. I didn't like Ed's bedroom furniture. I wanted mine. I had spent my first teaching paycheck on that furniture, and then I had spent hours at night staining, sanding, and then staining it again. My furniture was nicer, and it reflected me. Of course, I didn't know how to say any of this to Ed. I should have just said something, anything. Instead, I waited for him to read my mind. I would go to sleep with tears on my face, wanting my home back.

Then one day I did it. I insisted his furniture go. We placed an ad, and it sold in a few days. Once again the forklift was called into duty, and my bedroom set was brought upstairs. This time it wasn't a sad experience. A part of me would soon be in the house. I could finally claim a room as ours.

"But as for me, my prayer is to You, O LORD. At an acceptable time, O God, in the abundance of Your steadfast love answer me in Your saving faithfulness." (Psalm 69:13)

A new home. A new family. Each boy would have his own room, and Ed would have a reasonable drive to work. There were many things to be happy about as Diana watched the movers load her family's treasures. But she crouched in the window, knees to chest, tears flowing. The sting of loss was sharp, even as Diana began this new chapter of her life.

A paradox for many blended families is the fact that amidst the joyful new beginning, the sense of grief and loss for what was and is no more is often keenly felt. Diana had an identity: John's wife and widow, the teacher living in the nineteenth-century farmhouse, Ben and Josh's mom. Ed had an identity: Debbi's caring husband, widower, young Andy's dad, independent businessman, living in the four-bedroom home he had built. With Ed and Diana's marriage, what among those identifying elements would remain?

It is normal to miss certain aspects of significant relationships and people when those relationships end. As our lives change, we may experience a sense of losing pieces of ourselves because part of our identity is connected to those relationships we've known, those places we've loved, roles we've held, and things we've held dear. Diana speaks of her struggle to infuse her unique identity into a home in which her new spouse and his late wife had lived, and her tears fell as she left the 1800s limestone farmhouse behind.

Many couples choose to settle in neutral territory, a home new to all, which makes the boundary between the old and new clearer and the creation of new memories a little easier. This choice is recommended by Rev. Mark D. Wiesner, marriage and family therapist, who suggests that a new home places the two families on neutral turf.

However, moving to a home new to all family members may not be realistic. What then? A dialogue is necessary regarding what changes may occur in the home, who decides, what goes from home A to home B, and what does not. Be alert to the potential for unexpected emotions as you and your partner review the lives you lived before you became a couple. Your children are not immune to feelings of grief and loss and strong attachments to things that represent the previous family dynamic—things that remind them of other people they have loved. Be gentle with your children, with your partner, and with yourself.

Dealing with Grief and Loss

We all experience grief and loss. While our paths may be different and each experience unique, there are common themes shared by the brokenhearted. Sadness, loss of identity, disbelief, and the presence of physical, emotional, and spiritual symptoms are common themes. Bereavement is not the only time we experience grief and loss. Grief may accompany any type of significant loss: a job loss; divorce; relocation from one home, school, or town to another; or loss of physical ability and health.

Symptoms of Normal Grief

Grief is experienced in many ways and affects individuals in multiple areas of their lives. The extensive list of symptoms consistent with normal grief includes the following:

- Feelings: anger, sadness, guilt, anxiety, fear, loneliness, fatigue, helplessness, shock

- Physical sensations: tightness in chest or throat, dry mouth, breathlessness, weak muscles, lack of energy

- Thoughts: disbelief, confusion, preoccupation, difficulty concentrating

- Behaviors: sleeplessness, loss of appetite, crying, sighing, social withdrawal, restless over activity, dreams of the deceased, nightmares, and listlessness

"When my spirit faints within me, You know my way!"
(Psalm 142:3)

4

World's Biggest Garage Sale Hits the Neighborhood

My clothes took up little space inside the huge bedroom closet in Ed's house. Everything else I owned sat in boxes, waiting in the garage for Ed and me to make decisions.

My couch squatted where a car should be parked, barely visible under boxes of my precious belongings. The desk my mom lovingly restored for me when I began writing hunkered in the corner, piled with dishes instead of pages of a novel in progress. The upside-down lid of the popcorn popper accused me of neglect as we missed our late night movies together.

Something needed to be done. The garage had to be breaking some part of the fire code. Andy wanted his skateboard, and I couldn't find it. We couldn't even get to the bicycles to ride them. Forget pulling the minivan in out of the weather!

I felt like Lot's wife, traitorously thinking about the home I left behind. Did my children feel as displaced as I did? It was like being on vacation or visiting relatives—enjoyable, but you can't wait to get home to your own bed. Except this vacation had turned into a place where the sun didn't shine, the bed sheets were too short, and the water tasted funny.

Along with too many memories lurking around the corners of the house, the garage now housed boxes and extra furniture. Between us, we could open a resale store. I'm not too shallow to admit that in times of deep stress, I cling to my belongings. I had already given up my 1850s farmhouse, and I didn't want to part with anything else. But what can you do with two kitchen tables when you don't have a basement?

The only reasonable answer was to hold a garage sale. A big one. We took inventory and decided what would fit in Ed's house. We applied neon stickers to the rest at a price that couldn't reflect the attached memories.

What price can you put on your life? I stood knee-deep in boxes, duplicates of things that already clogged the cabinets and closets of the house I had moved into. My dishes, silverware, tablecloths, and even my desk had to go. I couldn't find a place to put the desk, and it seemed reasonable to sell my pots and pans because his were better.

It should have been okay to part with my bookshelves full of books. Unless I wanted to sell one of the boys and use his room, there wasn't a place for the books. Besides, did I really need my textbook from adolescent psychology? I stuck the yellow sticker on the cover. Too bad I didn't have a book on how to sell your junk and still keep your memories.

CINDY

"We had so many nice things after our wedding that we were able to sell a lot of our old stuff. I'm so glad eBay exists! I didn't want to have a tag sale. It takes so much time, and then there are the memories to deal with all day long as you wait for things to sell. What I couldn't auction off I gave to the local thrift store."

JENNIFER

"If I could do things over, I would have insisted we move to a house new to the both of us. My first five years and counting have been filled with begging to change things to reflect me and not his ex-wife."

Every day for weeks I looked at my treasures and attached the stickers. The silverware my mom received when she got married was tied in a ribbon and priced. I wanted to keep the set, but there wasn't enough room in the kitchen drawer. I was beginning to feel like there wasn't room for me in this house either. Maybe I could live in the garage? A tsunami of tears was building. I rushed upstairs into the master closet where no one could see me cry.

Ed found me and pulled me into his arms. With his hand, he brushed the back of my hair: "Tell me what's wrong."

"I'm homeless. I don't fit here. It doesn't feel like my house."

"So why aren't you making it into our home?"

"I'm afraid to change something you and Andy don't want changed. What if I took something off the wall that helps Andy remember his mom?" I blubbered more of my concerns on the front of Ed's shirt. This was his and Debbi's home, not mine, with her décor and decorative belongings lined evenly on the mantel. I didn't feel like the house could ever be my home.

It took a minute before Ed deciphered the language of tears. "It's our home now. Not mine and Debbi's. It belongs to you, me, and the boys."

Several months later, we were all in the van coming back from a fun-filled day. Everyone was tired, especially me. I glanced over at Ed and said, "I can't wait to get home."

His eyes gleamed. "Do you know what you just said?"

"I want to go home?" Was he losing his hearing?

"Yes, you said *home*, not back to *your house*." He smiled. "It makes me happy to hear you call our house *home*."

"He . . . set my feet upon a rock, making my steps secure."
(Psalm 40:2)

Combining households is stressful. If moving and blending households were easy, maybe we wouldn't find ourselves sobbing on the kitchen floor at 3 a.m. But some things don't blend. Two tables don't morph into one. Husband and wife must decide what to keep and what to place in the garage sale. Let's face facts: one or both spouses, and likely one or both sets of children, will have to move. The physical process of combining two households into one can be fraught with difficulty. Let's start with some practical tips to consider.

Before You Move

- Weed out the items you don't use, that don't work, or you don't like. You can have a garage sale; list items on eBay or Craigslist; or donate them to Goodwill, Salvation Army, or another charity.

- De-clutter. My Aunt Marilyn, age 80, is the queen of organization. She regularly de-clutters and says, "If I haven't used it or worn it in a year, out it goes."

- Use "our" stuff. Survey respondent Heidi reported that she and her husband had no problems eliminating duplicates or old items in favor of the "good" ones. Heidi and Tim's wedding gifts enabled them to replace "yours" and "mine" with "ours."

- Children can help pack their own rooms. Preschoolers may only manage one box with Mom or Dad's help but will feel some ownership of the process of moving.

- Label boxes lined with garbage bags as "Keep," "Give Away," and "Throw Away." All family members, even kids, can implement this sorting method.

GARAGE SALE POINTERS

- Strength in numbers: Joining forces with friends and neighbors will draw more traffic to your driveway. You can also share costs (e.g., advertising and table rental).

- Curb appeal: Clean items in good repair will attract shoppers. Arrange items so they can be viewed easily. Think of how they might be displayed in a store, and try to arrange something similar. Place toys on a blanket or low table away from breakables.

- Pricing: Mark items clearly. Use masking tape or stickers with good adhesive. You can even purchase pre-marked garage sale stickers at your local discount store. Consider one price for "like" items (e.g., all books 50 cents). Pricing items in quarter increments will make it easier to make change, enabling young children to help with the sale.

- Cash on hand: Start your day prepared with:
    One roll of quarters
    Twenty $1 bills
    Five $5 bills
    Four $10 bills

- City ordinances: Know your city's regulations regarding signage. Can you post signs on public streets? Are permits required?

- Time: Most buyer traffic occurs between 8 a.m. and 2 p.m. If you advertise an opening time, be prepared for early birds. Serious garage sale shoppers are out early trying to beat the competition.

Packing Tips

- Pack the kids' rooms last, especially younger children. This allows children a familiar place while you are doing the work of packing.

- Fill a backpack or suitcase with favorite books, stuffed animals, or games, so your child has these cherished items readily available, even during the chaos of unpacking. Do this for each child.

- Keep track of the items you pack in a notebook or computer file. Number each box and catalogue its contents. Do not write "Grandma's China" or "Video Game System" on the outside of the box. Rather, mark the box with a number and the room to which it should be delivered. For example, "14—Family Room." This makes the identification of valuable items more difficult for those who might steal.

- When packing your everyday dishes and glasses, slip them into baggies or plastic bags from the grocery store before you wrap them in paper. This adds some cushioning and keeps the dishes clean. The bags can be reused after unpacking.

- Utilizing boxes of uniform size makes loading the moving van or truck easier. Most households require three or four different box sizes to accommodate the variety of household treasures.

- Keep a bag of paper plates, napkins, and plastic cutlery handy. The day you unload at your new home, you'll have the items available for a picnic of deli sandwiches, take-out chicken, or peanut butter and jelly sandwiches. Everyone will need a break, and bodies don't stop requiring food during busy moving days. Sit down with your family, and thank God for your new beginning.

- Books should be packed in small boxes. Boxes designed to hold books and heavy items are available from moving and storage companies and some business supply companies.

- Using professional movers to pack and move? Be sure to clearly mark fragile items and heirlooms or they may not be covered by your agreement with the carrier. Designate a box or two of items to move yourself—especially items you may want immediate access to during the move. Move jewelry and valuables in a suitcase that you keep with you.

- When loading the moving van, load the kids' rooms last.

- Special consideration regarding the transport of family pets is important. If your cat or dog hasn't ridden in a vehicle for a long period of time, do a trial run for a short distance to determine how well your pet handles the potential stress of a longer trip. Veterinarians can make suggestions for handling your pet and even prescribe medications that enable pets to tolerate traveling more easily. If your moving situation precludes you from keeping your pets, thoughtful consideration regarding adoption is critical. Be prepared for significant grief experienced by family members who must separate from beloved pets. Because the loss of a pet can be traumatic, adding this dynamic to the blending mix should be avoided if possible.

Upon Arrival

- Unpack children's rooms first. Permit children to do as much of this as possible if they are old enough. Children feel more settled if they can personalize their rooms.

- The family kitchen is the next priority. Establishing routines helps a family adjust to change more easily. Family meals are important for family health and well-being, both physical and emotional.

- Children who do not live with you full-time need their own space too. Even if another sibling shares the room, a child will feel more secure if he or she has a drawer or two reserved for just him or her, a wall for posters, and a shelf for trophies and pictures. Your visiting children and stepchildren will feel more a part of the family when they know at each visit that their belongings will be just as they left them previously.

- Meet your neighbors. Questions such as, "When does the mail come?" can break the ice and give you helpful information. Be on the lookout for bikes and skateboards in neighbors' yards. Meeting kids their own ages will help your children feel better about moving.

- Thank God for your family's new beginning.

YOURS + MINE = OURS

You've sorted, weeded, packed, and unpacked. Maybe you had a garage sale before or after the move or listed items on eBay. Now, how do you make this house "ours"? Decorate your home in ways that reflect you and your spouse as a couple. Very few couples can afford to replace all home furnishings with new items. Decorating with pictures of the two of you and your children, items from your respective previous homes that you both agree on, and a few new things here and there can begin the transformation to "ours."

Keep a cool head during the transformation process. Redecorating isn't always joyous, as Lynn discovered. She told me her decorating style clashed with her new husband's old bachelor décor. She summed it up with, "I'm Mikasa and kid toys. He had no style."

Lynn's husband's "art" collection had to go. He collected glasses from every restaurant he visited, plastic and glass. But that's not the worst. His prize possession? A ceramic man with gigantic feet and long legs.

"This thing had a bulbous nose and ceramic whiskers protruding from its chin!" She told him he could keep it, but it had its own special storage place—a dark corner of the closet. Her reasoning for removing the statue? God made women nurturers and nesters, so they must be comfortable in their everyday surroundings to be happy.

In truth, the goal is for all family members to be comfortable in everyday surroundings, so each feels ownership of the home and that the home is "ours."

"God settles the solitary in a home." (Psalm 68:6)

5

Your Church, My Church, or a New Church?

I had been attending the same church since I was four years old. It had started out as a very small church, and as I grew, so did St. Mark's. It was a part of my life: I substitute taught there, attended many Bible studies, and I met my best friend for life in the pews.

The congregation at St. Mark's had become family. When John died, I was surrounded by brothers and sisters who offered comfort, food, grass cutting, and even help finishing Ben and Josh's bedroom that John had begun right before he died. Getting to church from our new home in Illinois was impossible. Getting three boys ready, one of them unwilling to get out of bed that early, became a difficult chore. One Sunday would slip by, and then another, and soon it was months since we had been to church. We had to do something about finding a church closer to home.

Ed belonged to the United Church of Christ, and I was Lutheran. I wanted Ben and Josh to remain Lutheran. Ed hadn't been attending a church, so he wasn't opposed to letting us follow in that denomination.

The hunt began. I wanted to find a church similar to the one I had left. I was looking for opportunities to connect with other Christian moms, a Bible study, and a church home that would welcome the attendance of three restless boys during the service. There were two possible Lutheran churches close to us. One wasn't the same Lutheran denomination that I had belonged to, but it had what I was looking for—lots of moms and activities for the boys and for Ed and me. I couldn't do it though. The doctrinal differences between that church and my Synod concerned me.

We tried the other church, which was located next to a small amusement center. The boys thought it would be fun to go to church there, and then after church, they could ride the bumper boats. For some reason we never did do that—something to do with being dressed for church?

We stayed at that church for awhile. I joined the women's group that was just getting started. There weren't any moms my age. We attended services, and it was implied that parents with children should sit in the back three rows. We tried that. This church dismissed by rows, from the front to the back. By this time, I was recognizing signs of attention deficit hyperactive disorder in Andy. Sitting in the back was difficult for him—there were so many children around us that he was unable to focus and sit still. It seemed to take a year for the older talkative adults to file down the aisle. By then, containing Andy in the pew was like trying to put toothpaste back in the tube.

We broke the unwritten rule the next week and moved closer to the front, even though the usher mentioned to us that we would probably be more comfortable in the back rows. Sermon time rolled around. Having been a teacher for learning-disabled and behavior-disordered students, I knew if I gave Andy some quiet activity to do, he would be able to sit still and absorb some of what was said from the pulpit. I had to be fair to the other two boys, though, so I pulled out three small notebooks and pencils and handed one to each son. I was right. Ed and I were able to listen, the boys were quiet, and I relaxed, knowing there wouldn't be a long wait at the end of the service for us to get out of the sanctuary.

As we left, the older couple behind us informed us that the back pews were reserved for those with children. I'm sure they thought they were being kind, letting us know there was a plan set in place where parents would be comfortable. I told them we wanted to sit up front, so the boys wouldn't be distracted by others. The woman's lips settled into a tight line, and then she said, "Well, we were distracted by them. Children shouldn't be drawing pictures of airplanes during the sermon."

I'm not sure how nicely I responded, but I know anything I learned about grace in the sermon no longer resided in my heart.

Later, Ed and I discussed whether to go back. Neither of us felt wanted at the church, and we knew our children didn't feel welcomed either. A few weeks later, the pastor visited us, as well as one of the women from the newly formed women's group. We decided to try it again. Once more, the congregation ignored us, other than to tell us that parents and children had reserved rows in the back. We didn't go back. We didn't go anywhere. Ed suggested going to his old church. I didn't want to, so we remained churchless instead going back to my home church when we could get everyone ready early enough.

Then one day, Ed saw an ad in the newspaper about a new Lutheran mission church. It was meeting in the storefront in our hometown. We were excited! Here was a chance to start our new life with a brand-new congregation! I prayed we would find people our age, people with children, and a church where children were welcomed in the front row.

Sunday came, and we arrived. A few anxious faces greeted us. We were welcomed along with a few other families that had seen the ad. Later, we were told they were afraid no one would come. There were several rows of folding chairs set up, and no one told us where to sit. The new congregation was young, there were children about the same age as ours, and everyone was friendly.

We had found a new home! We're still at that church, but now there is a real building—the storefront grew too small to contain the growing congregation and the massive amount of children. Our church makes sure we have greeters at the door to talk to the new people who come. Ed became a member while we were at the storefront and has served on many committees. And me? I found lots of new friends who have helped me through some rough times.

"The Lord your God is in your midst,
a mighty One who will save;
He will rejoice over you with gladness;
He will quiet you by His love;
He will exult over you with loud singing." (Zephaniah 3:17)

ON CHRIST THE SOLID ROCK WE STAND

Diana's faith was important to her. She and Ed agreed that church membership was a given, but they learned that finding the church that was the best fit for their family required ongoing discussion and perseverance.

Retired pastor F. Dean Lueking stresses the importance of a faith community:

> *Meaningful worship and service in the congregation is vital to making your household a place where God is at work in the daily rounds of your life together. The word you hear and the sacraments you receive equip you to love each other in spite of faults and failings that inevitably appear as the ups and downs of life come along. . . . Talk about how you see connections between Sunday worship and weekday life fit together.*[1]

Our families are strengthened through worship. God feeds us through His Word. The fellowship with other believers supports and encourages us in good and bad times. Because of Christ's death and resurrection, we are renewed, restored, and offered forgiveness and the hope of eternity. Finding a place to receive the Sacraments, celebrate God's gifts, worship, pray, and study Scripture shouldn't be that hard. But, as Ed and Diana found, it can be difficult.

Ed and Diana's search for a church was fraught with obstacles. Some of those obstacles came from within the family, while others were external. Preparation at the front end can minimize the number of obstacles we encounter. Calling the church or checking church Web sites to get as much information as possible ahead of time gives us an idea of what to expect. Most sites post a lot of information, including doctrinal beliefs, staff size and experience, ministry opportunities, and service times and style.

Mary Fairchild encourages us to consider the following before we begin visiting churches:

- What denomination are we looking for?
- What do we believe?
- What type of service structure do we prefer?
- Are we more comfortable with a particular worship style?
- Do we feel comfortable in a large congregation or a small one? Each size of congregation has different benefits and challenges.
- Is my family looking for a formal or casual atmosphere? The atmosphere may impact the manner in which most congregants dress for worship.[2]

KATHERINE

"We were Protestant but attended different churches. At first, the family attended both churches, but gradually my church became the family's home parish. Worship has been a very important part of my life. My relationship with Christ brought me a deep joy that I wanted for my children. Even so, I experienced frustration when I found myself having to wake my family members and make them get up for worship. After one such Sunday, I told my family that I would go with them to their church if they got up in time. Otherwise, I was going to my church, and anyone who wanted to accompany me was welcome. Eventually, the whole family attended with me, sharing the faith that sustained me."

Questions to discuss as your family begins the search for a church home:

- Are the church teachings biblically sound? Is the church's doctrine clear?
- Is the mission of this church clear?
- Does the church offer instruction for all family members (i.e., adult classes, Sunday School for kids, confirmation for all ages, Bible studies and fellowship activities for all ages)?
- How do clergy and congregation members welcome us? Do we feel like outsiders, or can we picture our family participating in the church and its activities?
- Are the church facilities compatible with my family's needs?

CHECK WITH THE KIDS!

Often kids will notice things we adults overlook.

• Do your kids feel welcome?

• Are there other kids in your son or daughter's age group?

• Are Sunday School rooms well lit and easy to find?

• Are teachers friendly?

A simple "What did you like best?" is a good conversation starter that can help us learn what our children noticed.

A church home is an important part of family life. But the first place our children learn about their Savior is, or should be, in their real homes, from us.

Survey respondent Mary shared some important reminders of the faith that sustained her:

> *Prayer is the thing. I spent a lot of time in prayer. I didn't know how to meet daily mountains and molehills. Every day presented new challenges. God saw us through. I received counseling from a psychologist and guidance from my pastor, friends, and family from time to time. I took it all in and sorted it out through prayer. I kept what I could use and forgot the rest. I never asked God why. I knew why! I loved my family and needed them. They loved me and needed me. Bible reading and Bible study brought me closer to God and gave me peace and strength.*

Church is important. The faith and Christian virtues demonstrated in our homes should be consistent and in harmony with what we learn when we attend church, Sunday School, and weekly Bible studies. Let your homes be the first place those seeds of faith are planted and nurtured.

> *"Teach me Your way, O Lord, and lead me on a level path." (Psalm 27:11)*

6

Pediatricians, Pediatric Dentists, and Pets, Oh My!

The excitement of living in a new place was wearing off for all of us. It had been two months since we started our new life. At first, it had been fun to experience all the new things the area had to offer, like going to the park and riding our bikes around town. Then it was August, and back to school brought new challenges.

It was time to get all of Ben's required physical checkups for school. Andy had been going to a well-recommended and respected pediatrician, so I decided to continue taking the boys there. Ed and several of the moms he knew highly recommended this doctor. He had a large practice and was known for his medical expertise. It all sounded good to me. What mom doesn't want her children seen by the best doctor in town?

After our first visit with this doctor, I wanted to go home, back to my little town where the pediatrician was nice and would look me in the eyes and offer his wisdom or comfort if needed. The new doctor was arrogant, and with his stiff shoulders and lack of a smile, let me know he didn't appreciate being questioned. He treated the boys and expected me to follow orders without any explanation. For some reason, it seemed I wasn't worthy of his knowledge.

Ben and Josh's old doctor didn't make me feel foolish when I called in a panic because Ben was having headaches. I knew he had just eaten ice cream, and it was likely caused by that, but I had lost John to a brain tumor, so I wasn't taking any chances. That doctor had listened and said I was not crazy. He affirmed that it was good to be aware of changes in my child's behavior. I liked him—a lot.

I wanted to change doctors, but didn't know where to go. I could keep the doctor in Missouri, but having a pediatrician over an hour's drive away seemed a disaster waiting to explode all over the backseat. I knew I didn't want to drive that far when one of them had an ear infection or worse. So we stayed with Andy's doctor.

Then it was time to make an appointment with the pediatric dentist. Andy had been seeing one locally, and Ed felt he was a good one. After my experience with the pediatrician, I wasn't quite ready to believe him.

"But I don't want to go to another dentist." Ben stood, legs hip width apart and arms crossed. "Everything is different. I want to go home."

Like Ben, I was feeling a bit uneasy about all the changes. Did I want a replay of the pediatrician visit? No. I had had enough.

Ben had given up his home, his friends, his school, frequent visits with grandparents, and our dog. Andy had his home invaded by us, but his social life hadn't changed much. Josh, at only three years old, didn't factor into the decision.

I didn't feel switching Andy to a new dentist would be a problem. Andy disagreed. He wanted to stay at his dentist. Ed and I discussed keeping Andy at his pediatric dentist while letting Ben and Josh continue with theirs. I couldn't see the benefit. It was much easier to take them all at the same time. Ben and Josh's pediatric dentist had his office set up to take multiple children at the same time for cleanings. Josh would get to go in with his big brothers, and I felt comfortable knowing all of them were able to see one another since parents weren't allowed in the back with their children. Plus, as an added joy, my sister-in-law scheduled her children at the same time, so we could take the kids out to lunch after the office visit. Ben and Josh would get to see their aunt and cousins, and Andy would get to know his new family better.

Decision made. We switched.

Now making choices about medical professionals the children would see a few times a years was easy compared to difficult choices about pets.

Blending families isn't only about blending humans. We had animals. I had a Doberman, Sally, who wasn't well, and she didn't like children or most people. One day, Andy, eager to see Ben and Josh, rushed through the door before I had a chance to secure the dog. The dog bit Andy in the arm; thankfully, he was wearing a heavy coat.

At my Missouri home, Sally was never allowed to play with my children without me after she bit Ben when he was two. She was part of the family but kept locked behind a gate on the stairs away from them when not supervised. Sally was afraid of kids, and I knew I couldn't bring her to live with us. The house didn't have a fenced yard, and she was dangerous. She had been seriously mistreated before John and I took her in to live with us. I couldn't find anyone willing to take her, except someone who wanted to leave her outside to guard a junkyard. I couldn't do that to her. I felt I had no choice but to put her to sleep. It was a difficult decision to make. I couldn't give her to someone who would try to make her even meaner, and with her illness, she wasn't an easy dog to keep inside.

Then there were the cats. Between us, Ed and I had four cats, two males and two females. My two cats were indoor cats, and Ed's cats were allowed outside. We kept my cats, Chuck and Loretta, at my home in Missouri until we moved my furniture. There wasn't an easy way to introduce them to Hulk and Psyche. Ed's house didn't have a basement, and all of the rooms were inhabited. So we hoped for the best and opened the cages. Surprisingly, chaos didn't happen. Those cats blended better and faster than the humans in our house.

Still, having cats didn't seem like enough. We needed a dog. The kids agreed a dog would be good. Ed didn't share the same excitement at the idea and said, "No dog."

For a while we listened to him. Then one day a new friend of mine took me to her neighbor's home. The woman wanted to sell her son's collie. The Lassie look-alike stole my heart, but I knew this was a dog that would be expensive. There would have to be visits to the groomer, and I could imagine the amount of vacuuming it would take having her in the house.

All three boys loved the dog and were asking if we could take her home. I was about to tell them no when the dog licked the owner, who then smacked the dog. The dog, Ginger, came home with us. I called Ed and said, "We have a collie. You're going to love her. Would you please pick up the dog's house from her old owner on your way home?"

Ginger never spent another night in that doghouse; we sold it at a garage sale. And yes, Ed did love her, and she attached herself to him, becoming his dog. She, too, blended well with our other pets.

Of course, you can't have just one dog for three boys. Soon Pebbles, an imitation Norfolk terrier, came to visit. She needed a home, and she got one. What's one more animal when you already live in a zoo?

*"Surely then you will lift up your face without blemish;
you will be secure and will not fear. You will forget your
misery; you will remember it as waters that have passed away."
(Job 11:15–16)*

Blending families requires many adjustments. Sometimes practical decisions, such as choosing new doctors and dentists, creep up on us. When someone becomes ill, and our doctor of choice is two hundred miles away, we remember that we have to make changes. Of course, selecting a doctor or dentist before you actually need one is preferred, but often parents find themselves trolling the local yellow pages while their son or daughter howls from the agony of an ear infection or abscessed tooth. Spouses are sometimes bitterly surprised to learn that changes in other peripheral relationships, like those with medical personnel, also bring a sense of loss.

Preparing a file of resources is helpful for blending spouses who will move to new communities. A directory containing important numbers kept near your primary phone, as well as programming them into your cell phone, can be a time-saver. Include emergency contact numbers (e.g., EMT, fire, and police department) along with family physicians and local hospitals. These numbers need to be easily accessible to all family members. It is a big help if you don't have to hunt for numbers for babysitters, schools, teachers, local church and pastor, and your favorite pizza parlor.

Before you move, prepare a picture book, or go online and check out a community Web site. This can help familiarize family members with their new community. Sharing photos of the parks, schools, and community resources can reduce fears and help family members picture themselves living in a community. Reassuring your children that your new town has tae kwon do, piano teachers, and skating rinks can make it seem a little more like home. If possible, drive through the town, and show them the facilities and parks.

Neighbors and friends are excellent sources of referral information. They can point you to daycare programs, tutors, and other tried and true helpful resources. Following one of my family's moves, a couple of women from our church took me under their collective wing, introducing me to their favorite hairdresser, dry cleaner, bakery, pediatrician, and dentist, and even suggested the best kindergarten teacher for my spirited youngest child. My friends told me what to expect from the different area physicians, so I could select the one that would best fit my needs. They had both lived in the community for a few years, were careful consumers, and had good reasons for their opinions and their choices. These friends saved me a lot of trial, error, time, and money.

Even with good referral resources, these new beginnings are stressful for most of us. Visiting a new physician or hairdresser for the first time can make blood pressures and anxieties rise. These are normal responses. Talk to your spouse regarding changes before the fact. Often the parent who will be doing most of the transporting to and from the various appointments may have a stronger voice in the selection process. Then, if you are making changes in established relationships, give your kids a heads-up regarding the changes. Be positive when explaining the shift.

If your children are changing schools, visiting the school prior to your son or daughter's first day of class will go a long way toward lowering anxiety. If your child will ride the bus, walk him or her to the bus stop and then back home to establish a sense of familiarity. If your child is a walker, walk the complete route with him or her, round-trip. Depending on your child's age and developmental abilities, you might need to do this several times before you and your child feel secure. Also, make a trip to the school and let your child walk the school's halls. Find the classroom and introduce him or her to the teacher. Locate important places like the cafeteria, restrooms, and drinking fountains.

Gather information: When are recesses and lunchtime? What are the school policies regarding dress codes, absences, tardiness, inclement weather, and school closures?

Diana, Ben, and Josh experienced many changes. They transitioned to a new community, a new home, and a new family. Andy also adjusted to a whole new family in his home and the need to share his dad. That was something he didn't have to do much in his past, especially after Debbi became ill. Ed was busy trying to smooth out the family members' challenges, even as he made his own adjustments. All the family members were making changes, adjusting, and learning new rules. But all the family members also loved the newest additions to the household, Ginger and Pebbles. The gentle collie and the imitation Norfolk terrier acted like a magnet, pulling the family members together.

> "O LORD, You will ordain peace for us, for You have indeed done for us all our works." (Isaiah 26:12)

7

What's in a Name?

About a month before our wedding, we took the kids to hike the trails at Giant City in southern Illinois. I had followed Ed and squeezed under a large, gray granite boulder that hung over our heads. The boys, being smaller, seemed to be miles away. I started after them in haste. Ed grabbed my hand: "Wait, they'll be okay. There's something I wanted to talk to you about."

"What?" I kept a close watch on the boys, my foot inching forward.

"Are you going to keep your name, or will you take mine?"

Thoughts flew like fireworks in my brain. Why hadn't I thought about this aspect of marriage? I had been practicing writing Lesire since I was sixteen, and then I only was able to use it for nine years. I liked it so much better than my maiden name. "Why do you ask?" I hoped to stall for a moment to separate my past from my future.

"I don't think my mom will understand if you don't take the Brandmeyer name, that's all."

"I can't change Ben and Josh's name. It was really important to their dad that the name continue."

"Although I would like them having my name, I wouldn't want to take that from them," Ed said.

"And what about school forms? I would like Ben and Josh to have the connection of Lesire to me with their teachers. And my writing—I have things published with Lesire." I realized I no longer knew where the kids were, but this discussion was important, so I stayed in place. "And I want Andy to have a connection with me too. What if I just used Diana Lesire Brandmeyer as my name? Would that be okay?"

"Sure. Works for me." Ed flashed me a grin and kissed my forehead.

I sighed. This man is a gem. I knew in my heart how blessed I was going to be in this marriage. "Thanks. Now if I ever write a book and get famous, all the boys will be able to say, 'That's my mom. See? There's my name on the cover.'"

"I think that could happen."

Not only did he let me keep my name, but he believed in me!

We had been married four months and thought it was time to update our wills. Then we took it a step farther and decided to adopt each other's children. We didn't have to do that, but both of us wanted to. We felt if something happened to either of us, then our families would respect that the boys were legally brothers, consider them connected, and honor the bond.

Ed began checking out various lawyers to find out what the process would cost. The first lawyer's price was exorbitant. We assumed we had to close that door. We then instructed our families that our desire was for the children to stay together if something happened to us.

This was an issue that concerned us. The boys had already each lost a parent, and if they were to lose both Ed and me as well, the traumatic experience would be exacerbated with the breaking up of the new family. Ed and I knew there was a possibility that both of us could die; we had already had the unexpected happen to us, so we were determined to prepare for the future.

AMANDA

"When I found out I had cancer, we had to rush to get my ex-husband to let my husband have custody of my son. I was so afraid I was going to die, and his real dad, who hadn't shown any interest in him since he was born, would want to take him away from the only father he's ever known."

Ed and I kept our appointment with the lawyer who was preparing our will. She asked us about our sons and if we were going to do the adoption. Ed explained the lawyer he had spoken with had given him a cost we couldn't afford.

"Really? It couldn't be that much. There aren't any biological parents left to contest the adoption." She sat back in her chair and put her hands in her lap.

Ed told her the amount he had been quoted. "He said it would take almost a year to get in front of a judge."

Her eyes widened. "That much?" She scooted back to her desk, not looking at us for a minute while she shuffled through the papers in our file folder. Then she laced her fingers together and placed her hands on the folder. She said, "I can do it for much less. All I need are copies of the death certificates, and I'm certain we can do this next month."

"Well?" Ed looked at me. "What do you think?"

"I'm ready. I wish it could be sooner, but a month is better than never."

Our lawyer looked at both of us with a serious face. "Are you are sure this is what you want to do? You realize it is permanent; if your marriage is dissolved, you will still be the parents of these children, despite the fact they aren't biologically related?"

"Yes, of course we understand, don't we?" I looked at Ed for confirmation.

He nodded. "I'm ready."

Some may think we were naïve, but at that moment, we knew our marriage was going to last until God called one of us home.

Ed and I discussed how we would tell the kids. Were they old enough to understand what we were doing? Should we mention that it would help keep them together if something happened to us? Or would the thought of that make them feel insecure?

Ed came up with a plan so perfect it was as if he had reached into both of our hearts and minds and melded the best of our intentions together.

We herded the boys onto to the living room couch.

"Are we in trouble?" Andy's feet banged a rhythm against the bottom of the couch.

"No, you aren't in trouble," Ed said. "Mom and I want to talk to you about something serious."

Andy looked at the ceiling.

Ben traced the design on the couch with his finger.

Josh took some building blocks apart and began putting them back together.

"Nothing is wrong with us, boys. It's okay." I had a feeling they thought we were going to tell them either Ed or I was sick.

"Do you boys know what it means to be adopted?" Ed asked.

"When you don't have parents, you get adopted." Ben's eyebrows wrinkled. "Are we getting another kid?"

Ed laughed. "No. We want to make it official that we are a family."

Two of the three faces looked confused, and the youngest face appeared to be in a dream world.

"Boys, we have the opportunity to do something very special. Mom and I get to pick our kids, so Mom is going to adopt Andy, and I'm going to adopt Ben and Josh. That makes us legally responsible for you."

More confused looks.

"Next month, we are all going to go and stand in front of a judge. He's going to ask us if we really want you boys. Then the judge will ask each of you if you want us for parents," Ed said. "There will be one difference between our family and other families. Ben and Josh are going to keep their last names."

"Is mine going to change to Lesire?" Andy's body was moving up and down.

"No, Andy, you get to stay a Brandmeyer," said Ed.

"So, are we done?" Andy was already sliding off the couch, and Josh was following him.

Those two rushed off. Ben sunk against the back of the couch. Tears were starting to pool.

"Benjamin, what's wrong?" I asked.

"I want Dad's name."

"You get to keep Dad's name." As I said this, I knew this was the beginning of a new phase in our family.

"I want New Dad's name, not Old Dad."

Ed moved to sit next to Ben. "I would be honored to have you use my name, Ben. When you get older, though, I think you'll understand why we don't want to change it. You and Josh are going to carry on your father's name. That's a big deal when you are a man."

"But I want yours."

"I understand. What if you wait until you're sixteen, and then we can decide?"

"Can I just try it?"

Brilliant! I had a feeling about how this would end. "Of course! Let me get some paper, and you can practice writing it."

Pencil in hand, he wrote Benjamin John, then paused. "How do you spell Brandmeyer?"

I spelled it out for him, and he slowly wrote it. It looked strange on the paper to me: "Benjamin Brandmeyer." It wasn't the name chosen for him.

"Never mind." Ben tossed the pencil on the coffee table. "It takes too long to write. I only want to write Ben on my papers."

The official adoption day came. We stood in front of the judge. When the judge asked Andy if he wanted me to be his mom, I held my breath. I was sure he would say no.

"See what kind of love the Father has given to us, that we should be called children of God; and so we are." (1 John 3:1)

But Andy said yes! All the boys said yes! The adoption was complete and official, but the boys kept their names as they appeared on each birth record. Retaining their birth names was carefully considered. What might a name change mean as Ben and Josh grew to manhood? How might it impact their extended family? Would it change their connectedness to Ed or to John's family? These were deeply personal considerations.

For many readers, a name change is not an option. There are legal factors that make this consideration impossible, or perhaps your children are blessed with living biological parents who are emotionally invested in their children's lives. But some of you have walked a path similar to Diana and Ed's and experienced the pain of loss that accompanies bereavement. Others may have had earlier marriages scarred by abuse. Still others may have parented children alone due to the absence or neglect of the other biological parent. Until now.

Johnny Smith, Johnny Jones, or Johnny Smith Jones?

There is much debate surrounding legally changing children's names following remarriage. Factors to consider include:

- How will this change benefit my children?
- What are the motives behind the change?
- Will this strengthen or harm bonds with extended family?
- Do my children have opinions about the possibility of changing their names?
- Will a change of name enable my children to heal from the effects of abuse?
- Do my children know that they are loved unconditionally, regardless of their names?

- Are my children secure in their identity in Christ?
- Is a name change in my children's best interest?

Miss, Ms., or Mrs.?

Diana and Ed carefully considered how changing her name might affect her personally and professionally. Diana had established herself as a writer and was published under the name "Lesire." Navigating how she might retain that professional identity and honor her husband was a careful process. Also taken into account were the culture, rituals, and attitudes of their extended family.

Diana and Ed agreed that Diana would take Ed's last name but retain her boys' surname as her middle name. Some women who have "professional names" use their spouse's name in their private, day-to-day lives but are known in their businesses by that previously established professional name.

Other women take their husband's name as their last name but choose to continue use of the maiden name in that middle spot. But most women still opt for the traditional practice and use the husband's last name exclusively. For many, this cultural norm is still viewed as a means to show respect for the husband and acknowledge his leadership in the family.

Some women, like Lori, prefer to retain a last name that matches that of their biological children, often stating the concern that this practice may minimize confusion between school officials, teachers, community program directors, coaches, and the blended family. Lori expressed her belief that her children's sense of identity was more secure if she and the children shared the same last name, even after Lori remarried. Most school registration forms are crafted to make clear to school officials and teachers the name designations within a family system, including differences between parent, child, stepparent, sibling, and stepsibling.

Mom or Dad?

There are many points to weigh as a couple considers what legal choices are made regarding family members' last names. These are serious matters and warrant prayerful thought and respectful discussion. Equally important and challenging is determining what the children will call the newly married parents in the blended family home. Give children time to adjust to the new family dynamic before expecting to hear "Mom" or "Dad" applied to a stepparent.

During your courtship, they may have referred to you as "Miss Suzie" or "Mr. Don." Ed and Diana's sons easily came to recognize the stepparent as "Mom" and "Dad," but their other biological parents were deceased. Many children feel disloyal calling a stepparent "Mom" or "Dad" and never make the transition. The best they can manage is transitioning from "Miss Suzie" to "Suzie," and maybe when they have children to "Grandma Suzie."

MARY

Mary, a divorced mother of one, reported that her stepson proposed to her before she had a first date with his dad. She would later marry his dad, a widower and father of three. Mary allowed the children to call her by her first name, but the two younger ones almost immediately called her "Mom."

The oldest one, Jenny, age 15, called Mary by her first name until her grandmother encouraged the teen to call Mary "Mom." Jenny later told Mary that she had reasoned it was okay to call her "Mom" because Jenny had called her biological mother "Mama."

While the younger stepdaughter initially called Mary "Mom," Sandy began to give Mary problems after a year or so. When Mary probed, Sandy confessed she was beginning to love Mary too much, and it felt disloyal to her deceased mother. Mary reminded her stepdaughter that she loved Sandy's dad, her siblings, and Sandy. She assured the girl that there was enough love to go around and that she could never, and didn't want to, take her natural mother's place. "I told her it was okay to love me for me and to continue to love her birth mother too," Mary later recounted. Sandy said, "Okay," and that ended that.

Consider the following as you discuss how children in the blended family address stepparents:

- Age of children in the household. Younger children adjust more easily to referring to stepparents as "Mom" or "Dad."

- Desires of the biological parent. Is it necessary to hurt a biological mother or father's feelings by insisting that the children call you a name previously reserved for that parent?

- Loyalty issues. Children often feel that using the same term for both parent and stepparent is disloyal to the biological parent. A child's loyalty to his or her biological parent should be honored.

- Perhaps you feel strongly that children should refer to parents using terms that indicate a parental role and relationship. Consider permitting stepchildren to address you using "Mom Jones," "Mom Molly," or a form of parental address other than that used for the biological parent. If the biological parent is known as "Mom," perhaps you can be called "Mother," "Momma," or "Mom Molly."

R-E-S-P-E-C-T

Whatever terms are used to address family members on legal documents or in casual conversation, the demonstration of respect for one another is critical. A parent's behavior, including speech, is the model for the respect parents desire from their children and stepchildren. This includes interactions with former spouses, extended family, school officials, biological children, and stepchildren. Respectful interactions can be important factors in easing a child's adjustment to the new family dynamics and will encourage family members to address one another with affection, no matter what title or name is used.

Of greatest value is the identity we have in Christ: sinners saved by grace. Are we demonstrating God's love to our children through respectful words and actions toward all the people in our children's lives? Ask yourself the following questions. Do I honor Christ by:

- The manner in which I speak to my children and stepchildren?

- The way I speak and interact with other family members, including previous spouses and other stepparents?

- The words I use when speaking about others, especially former spouses and extended family members?

Parents are a child's first teachers. We have the privilege of modeling Christian love, repentance, forgiveness, and discipleship, and showing our children and stepchildren that our Father in heaven has limitless love for His sons and daughters. What is in a name? Family names, nicknames, and terms of affection are negotiable. The identity we have through Christ is not.

> *"I will be a Father to you, and you shall be sons and daughters to Me, says the Lord Almighty." (2 Corinthians 6:18)*

8

Who's Your Daddy?

There is something very different about being a parent of a child who isn't biologically yours. You have lots of love to offer, along with definite ideas on how you want this child to grow to maturity. You can even visualize the end result: It's a sunny afternoon in the spring, and your son is standing in front of a podium because he's valedictorian of a top-ten school. He's giving a speech unlike any ever given before by a student. You're sitting tall in your chair, clasping your husband's hand, so pleased that all has turned out so well. Then your son stops in the middle of his speech to do the thing all mothers want. He thanks you for all of your love and support, and he acknowledges he wouldn't be where he is today without you. Tears will, of course, stream prettily down your cheeks (without smearing your makeup).

I had big dreams.

The reality is I wasn't the only one who had dreams for him. In our family, there were a lot of parents with ideas on how the boys should be raised, and it seemed they all conflicted with one another.

Andy's aunt never minded telling me what her sister would have preferred for Andy. Then there was Debbi's best friend, who assured me Andy wouldn't have been able to get away with some of his behaviors if Debbi were here. There were babysitters who let him do things he shouldn't, and then there was Debbi herself. Wait, I know I told you she died when Andy was five. But the thing is, she was part of my parenting. She was a teacher, so I knew excellent grades would be something she desired. She had a great sense of fashion, so I knew she would want him dressed well for various occasions. What other things would she have wanted for her son? I felt compelled to try to figure out what would have been important for her and do it, and yet I wanted to claim him as mine only.

Ed had similar issues. He felt responsible for respecting John's heritage and what he would have taught Ben and Josh. And he had to fight me over some of those things. John liked guns. I did not. So the boys didn't learn to shoot a gun until after they left our home. John would have insisted the boys earn their own money to buy their first car. Ed wanted to buy them a car. We compromised by matching their savings up to a certain dollar amount. John loved horses and we had owned two, but Ed wasn't a horseman and didn't desire to be. Instead, on vacations when the opportunity arose, he gave the boys a chance to go horseback riding. He made sure he kept all of John's tools separate from his, so Ben and Josh could have them, or at least he tried to. Once Ben started using tools, they were all stuffed back into the same toolbox. Ben didn't care; he considered all the tools his dad's. Josh wasn't interested in tools: he had a dad and big brothers to help him fix things.

"Mom yells at me." Andy had a list of complaints to bring before Ed. Some of them were valid. I did yell a lot. And it seemed I yelled at him the most. It was one of those Sunday morning confessions I would have to ask forgiveness for every week.

Ed said it's because we are so much alike that we know how to irritate each other. I wasn't trying to irritate; I just wanted Andy to do what I asked him to do. Just once, without arguing with me.

This time I was up against a babysitter. I didn't believe Andy, but he insisted he was allowed to run through the house with a knife in hand to play ninja. He wanted to be realistic. Included with his list of complaints was the fact that his summer wasn't turning out like the one before we got married.

He was right.

Because Ed worked long hours, he wanted Andy's summers to be fun. He gave the babysitter money to take him somewhere almost every day. They went to the movies, bowling, the zoo, putt-putt golfing, and swimming. For a seven-year-old, I'm sure that summer was amazing. Then I came along with two other people who vied for attention, and I wasn't a babysitter. I was the mom. I came with chores to do, a budget to stick to, and a house to clean. Our fun activities were going to the library, the park, the pool, and the grocery store.

Ed calmly talked to Andy. He told him that now there were three children, and it was too expensive to do activities every day. He explained that normal families don't do fun things that cost money every day; instead they stay home and play with the toys and games they own.

Andy just wanted me to stop yelling so much. Ed said he would talk to me about Andy's concerns. In that moment, a pattern was set, one that would cause us many problems. Andy decided he would check with Ed about any decision I made if he didn't like mine.

What made parenting so difficult in this situation is that we didn't want to make John and Debbi look bad. Both of them had been ill, with some changes in personality, before they died. Many times they weren't able to be the best of parents, sometimes parenting with the level of expertise and attitude of a child.

We didn't want to bring memories of the bad times up with the boys. We also didn't want them to think their "old" mom and "old" dad were saints. It was impossible to be good parents with Debbi and John hanging around in our minds.

These two predecessors had to be cleaned out of our parenting closet. Ed didn't have as much difficulty doing this as I did. I was with the children more because I was a stay-at-home mom, and I was a woman. I invited input from people who had known and loved Debbi. And then it took me a long time to learn how to uninvite them. What I learned was that I had to trust my instincts. I was with Andy all the time; they were not. I was his living mom now, not Debbi. It was up to me, Ed, and God how well I parented my children.

"Make every effort to keep the unity of the Spirit through the bond of peace." (Ephesians 4:3)

Ah, triangles. The Holy Trinity is the perfect embodiment of an interconnected, complementary relationship.

When triangles occur in human relationships, however, the legs are mismatched and the sides out of balance. We will not find perfect interconnection and complementary response, even in healthy relationships. In her last statement, Diana draws a beautiful picture of the Brandmeyer marriage, with God as the base of a triangle, Diana and Ed as the sides. That is the prayer for all Christian couples.

However, the situations recapped earlier in the chapter will have mental health professionals thinking "triangulation," over and over again. Family therapists consider the notion of the triangle an important one. The concept of the triangle in family dynamics is not typically used to describe healthy interactions. A triangle can occur in a variety of ways but always involves two family members in alliance against or rejecting another family member. The alliances or oppositional connections are fluid and can shift as dynamics within the family change. In most families, these shifting alliances are perceived as positive—everyone gets a turn to be the one at odds. Believe it or not, this is preferred to a situation in which one family member is the scapegoat and always perceived as the problem in the family, rather than a symptom of difficulties that warrant change.

An enormous challenge for widows and widowers occurs when the deceased spouse in some fashion comprises one leg of a triangle. Though deceased, Debbi and John were both present in the ways Diana and Ed raised their boys. Education was important to Debbi, and John loved horses: these memories impacted Ed and Diana's interactions with and plans for their sons. Honoring a deceased loved one's desires and memory can be a very healthy endeavor.

Thinking of the deceased parent or spouse off and on throughout life is normal, especially during milestone events like confirmation or graduation. But sometimes the memory of a loved one takes on an unhealthy role in one's life, the deceased individual seeming all too real.

One survey respondent spoke of the "ghost" of her previous spouse, which was actually the impact of her memory of him and the manner that she felt directed by that ghost. Joy reported that her late husband's shortcomings seemed to fade with time, and his strengths seemed greater over time. Another respondent refused to let anyone sit in the recliner that had been her late husband's favorite. The behavior of retaining a deceased individual's possessions "ready for use," should he or she return, is referred to as "mummification" by mental health experts.

Children and adults alike may experience a sense that their loved one is watching over them. Mental health experts refer to this phenomenon as a "sense of presence." This "sense of presence" may help the bereaved to cope, or it may be disturbing. Perhaps there are unresolved issues pertaining to the deceased. Professional help or pastoral care and counseling can guide a bereaved individual toward healing.

The triangulation possibilities increase when all parents are living, and the family structure has changed because of divorce. One leg of the triangle can be siblings, stepsiblings, grandparents, other extended family, teachers, friends, or co-workers. We can enjoy healthy, supportive relationships with all of the aforementioned. But when we turn to a co-worker or a grandparent to process a situation that should first be discussed with our spouse, an unhealthy relationship triangle may result.

The exchange between Diana and Andy is a clear example of a triangle commonly experienced by blended families: a third person (Ed) is brought into a parent—child interaction (Diana—Andy) to form an alliance with one against another. The alliance here, between Ed and Andy in opposition against Diana, was one that occurred frequently—for awhile. Eventually Diana and Ed recognized how destructive this pattern of interaction was to their marital relationship and the family as a whole.

A triangle isn't always between a parent and child against another parent, as outlined in the possible triangle configurations. Suppose Diana had picked up the phone to call her best friend and complain about Ed's response to this or another situation. When Diana's friend joins her in opposition to Ed (alliance between Diana and best friend), another triangle is formed.

Addressing a concern biblically may resolve the situation before it becomes a conflict. Christ's words recorded in Matthew 18:15 read: "If your brother sins against you, go and tell him his fault, between you and him alone." God intends that we implement this process when we have been wronged (or believe that we have). First, you go to your spouse.

When a child comes careening down the hall with a complaint about his stepdad, your husband, remember the importance of the marital unit. Take a deep breath, and gather information from your spouse regarding the child's complaint. Resist the very strong pull toward triangulation with your child or with another. Stop and pray.

> *"Is anyone among you suffering? Let him pray."*
> *(James 5:13)*

Join hands with your husband or wife and pray. Use wise eyes to assess the resources He has placed before you, and take time determining the proper response to troubling times. As Diana wrote, "It was up to me, Ed, and God how I parented my children." And so it is for you. That doesn't mean you become closed to outside influences or isolated from others who have been important to you. But the place from which you begin and end remains Christ plus the spouse plus you. Notice there is not a designation of opposition in this triangle, but rather one of unity.

> *"There is one body and one Spirit—just as you were called to the one hope." (Ephesians 4:4)*

9

Good Night, Sleep Tight, Don't Let the Frustrations Bite

Was it wrong to pray for the sun to set, for darkness to fall, for an eclipse at 4 p.m.? I was exhausted. Why did we get married in summer? If we had waited until fall, I would only have had to wrestle two kids to bed in the summer. Three boys were much harder to take care of than I had imagined.

I flashed back to my previous life and let the memories simmer. Bedtime for Ben and Josh arrived early; they would both be in their beds by seven. Bath time would be over and *Goodnight Moon* read at least twice. Then the evening was mine, all mine, every minute to be used by me. I could read, paint my fingernails, or write without being disturbed. Delicious. *Mine, all mine*—I almost hugged myself with happiness at the thought.

The clock was my enemy. Had the boys superglued the hands in place? The last few minutes were torture, as the clock hands crept closer to the best time of the day. *Please God, let them want to go to bed tonight. I have this book I want to read—you know God, the one that I've been trying to read for weeks now?*

The clock chimed 7 p.m. Yes! I yelled from downstairs, "Get ready for bed!"

Feet pounded down the stairs, then a thud as he landed his trademark jump from the last two steps. Andy. It hadn't taken me long to learn he never walked at a slow pace anywhere. "Mom! Why do we have to go to bed now?"

"Mom! Does Josh have to take a bath first?" Ben called from upstairs; he had requested an elevator installed since taking the stairs was too much work.

"Mom! Mom! Mom!" Josh. He liked to say *mom*.

I loved that title, but right then I wanted to be Diana. Where did she go? Bedtime had become a circus. It would have been easier to insert a snake back into his skin than get all three boys under covers. I could get Josh into bed, and Ben would soon follow.

However, Andy and the word *bedtime* couldn't share the same airspace.

This is one of those things I should have realized before Ed and I married. He would call me at 11:00 p.m., and Andy would still be awake. "He's a night person, doesn't like to go to bed. Sometimes we go out at 8 p.m. and get ice cream or a snack at the mall. It's the only time of day I get to spend with him."

That made sense—then. Now things had to change. Our family had to establish a routine, or this mom wasn't going to make it until school started.

"Ed, we have to get the kids into bed every night about the same time."

"Why? It's summer."

"It will help them when it's time to go to school; they need the structure, especially Andy." At the word *structure*, Ed's eyebrow twitched. Would he support me on this?

"I don't think you can get Andy into bed before 11 p.m."

"I can if you help me. We need to do this for us too; we need to spend some time alone together." That stopped the eyebrow twitch.

"How are you going to do it? You can't put Josh to bed at the same time as Ben and Andy. He's younger. Andy won't like it if he has to go to bed at the same time as Josh."

"I know that."

"He's not going to want to go to bed early. Even when he was a baby, he wouldn't go to sleep until after midnight. This isn't going to be easy."

"I have a plan."

A month later, Andy and I called a truce. I would read to Josh, say prayers, and tuck him in for the night. Then I would alternate between Ben and Andy's room for the nighttime reading, tuck them into their beds, and say prayers with them. That worked for awhile until Andy said he didn't like the books I was reading. He wanted scary books.

Ben did not.

I tried to alternate reading to each of them from different books in their own room. It was exhausting. Who did I read to first, and what did I do when they each asked me to read longer? I gave up. I told the older two that they would be allowed to stay up as long as they were reading.

Ben went to sleep. Andy didn't want to read, so out went his light. A few hours later, before we went to bed, Ed and I would check on them, and Andy would still be awake.

Bedtimes were established, but bath time was another trial.

"I'm first."

"It's my turn to go first."

The ritual was the same every night; choose a kid to get in

the bath first. How do you decide? Andy would say, "It was my house first, so I get to go first." Ben would say, "I'm the oldest, so I get to go first." Ben was only twenty-one days older, so he didn't have a lot of power with those words. The argument raged overhead.

"How are we going to fix this, Ed? I can't take this anymore. The two of them fight over who's first all the time." I wasn't sure if the tension I felt could be restrained behind a nice mommy smile much longer. Evil Mom would come back from the honeymoon trip any minute now.

Ed must have sensed danger in the air. "Ben and Andy, get down here!"

Thump, thump, bump. Andy arrived. "What?"

Soft steps skittered down the stairs. Ben took in the look on his dad's face, his eyes grew larger, and he moved closer to me.

"Have a seat on the couch."

"Am I in trouble?" Andy bounced onto the couch.

Ben sat quiet, with his knees pulled into his chest, eyes moving between me and his dad, a bit fearful.

"No. You aren't in trouble. We're going to solve this bath time problem right now. Even or odd, what do you want to be?"

Both boys and I stared at him.

"Here's the deal. Andy, you were born on the twenty-ninth—you're going to be odd. Ben, you were born on the eighth—you'll be even. So every day you check the calendar; if it's an odd date, Andy, you will go first. Ben, if it's even, you go first. Get it?"

"Ed, they're eight. I don't think they understand even and odd numbers yet."

"Not a problem. We know, and they can learn." He yanked the calendar off the wall. He spent time teaching the boys, and then he hit a month that ended in thirty-one.

"So Andy gets to go first both days?" Ben asked.

Ed scratched his head. "No baths on the thirty-first of the month."

The boys cheered.

I couldn't wait until they left the room to express my thoughts on that declaration.

The method worked. We often heard claims of, "My day!" even in the college years. When they both had cars, they decided to use the same method to claim the empty space in the garage.

(Disclaimer: the boys took baths or showers on the thirty-first and first of the month—Mom's rule.)

The next battleground was the front passenger seat. The "my day" rule didn't work because some days we did a lot of driving and others none at all. I tried keeping track of who rode last, but couldn't always remember, which led to arguments. I could have had them all ride in the back, but that meant there would be touching, which would lead to more backseat arguments.

In desperation, I grabbed two wooden clothespins and wrote their names on them. I clipped them on the visor on the passenger side. When a child rode in the front seat, they moved their pin to the right of their brother's leaving a clear message of who would be riding in the front on the next trip. Leaving home with them became more pleasurable.

A challenge for me came when it was time for Josh to take a nap. He still needed naps, while Ben and Andy were past that stage. Yet I needed an afternoon break. Ben understood how naptime worked. He had to be quiet, so Josh could sleep. He had had a few years to understand. Often he would tell Josh he was taking a nap too; then he would sneak downstairs and play with his cars.

Andy didn't understand being quiet in his house. He had been the only child for eight years—no need to walk quietly down the stairs.

I still wanted to read a book to catch my breath, to make it through the rest of the day. After lunch became mandatory quiet time for the rest of the summer. The two older boys would practice their silent reading for a half hour in their rooms. Did they read? I don't know. They were quiet, Josh slept, and I was able to recharge for the rest of the day.

It troubled me that I seemed to be exhausted all the time. It didn't seem right that adding an extra child would cause such extreme tiredness. I had taught school and never felt this way. By the time school started that fall, I would fall asleep in the car while waiting for them to be excused for the day. I would drive home and need to rest.

After reading several parenting books, I realized I needed to take care of myself, or my family would continue to suffer. I went to the doctor, and after a blood test, I discovered I have hypothyroidism. The disease is easily treatable with a drug, and within six weeks Mom was back on her feet playing referee.

"And let the peace of Christ rule in your hearts, to which indeed you were called in one body. And be thankful."
(Colossians 3:15)

Children can bring joy, laughter, and excitement to a family. But it is not unusual for parents of young children to feel as Diana did: worn out, longing for adult companionship, lonely for their spouse on one hand, and like they have lost sight of their individuality on the other. Add to that the stress of new rules, new roles, sleep deprivation, and perhaps a medical condition that impacts one's stamina, and Mom or Dad may be creeping very close to meltdown territory. How do you conserve energy and carve out needed couple and individual time? Is it even possible?

TAKING TURNS

Nothing can wear down a parent and fray the nerves more than relentless bickering. Ed's creative bath time solution involved a procedure for turn-taking. It made sense to Andy and Ben and was easy to implement and remember. Taking turns is not just for children. Moms and dads can conserve parental energy by taking turns in application of discipline and in support of each other during stressful times. Frequently, a parent doesn't recognize the need for partner assistance until experiencing intense emotions. The even or odd approach to turn-taking is ideal for settling something like bath rotations or emptying the dishwasher, but it's hard to schedule when your parenting reserves will run low.

A parent's stamina is affected by many things:

- Job situation

- Personal energy level

- Method of coping

- Family dynamics, including support of extended family

- Conflict

- Medical concerns of nuclear and extended family
- Family and individual sleep patterns
- Mental health concerns
- Financial concerns
- Self-care: eating and exercise habits
- Living conditions in the home, including space and maintenance concerns
- Spiritual drought

Communicating with your spouse when you are nearing the point of overload is critical. This means letting your partner see your frailty and weakness so that you might avert a meltdown and restore your resources. Better yet, be proactive: adopt healthy self-care strategies, identify the resources God has provided, and evaluate your use of them.

Ed and Diana's collaborative and creative approach to parenting helped them conserve energy and carve out some time for themselves. And their boys were clean!

"Holiness befits your house, O LORD, forevermore."
(Psalm 93:5)

10

Who's in the Bedroom?

Blending a family isn't just about smoothing out the lumps with the kids. Mom and Dad have to blend their pasts with their present if they are going to have a successful marriage. That means no former spouses allowed in arguments, expectations, and personalities. This is not an easy thing to accomplish when you are working to establish a strong family structure as well.

The first time Ed entwined his fingers through mine, my body betrayed me. I was a teenager with hormones sending flares to heaven. His hardworking hands were rough against my smooth skin. My breath quickened, and I was ready to fall in love—physically. Mentally, I had to make major mind shifts. Ed's hand didn't feel like John's. When Ed hugged me, my head didn't seem to sit as easily against his chest. This was a good thing. It made it easier to extinguish some of those fireworks that were leading me where I wasn't quite ready to go. Knowing that God made woman to be with man made sense when I was with John. But what about now? Had God made me to be with another man as well? Was I betraying John by falling in love with Ed? Could I ever achieve the same, or an even better, level of intimacy with Ed?

I knew if I were comparing how it felt to be with Ed against John's memory, it would be wise to take this part of our relationship slowly. I wanted to belong totally to Ed when the time came.

❧

About a month before the wedding, Ed asked, "Remember when we were on your porch swing last summer, and you said it felt like John was sitting there with us?"

"I do. It was an odd feeling. We weren't really dating, and yet to me it felt like John was here protecting what was his. Did you feel like that too?"

"Yes. And because we were talking about her so much, it felt like Debbi was there too."

"Why are you asking now?"

"I wanted to see if you feel differently now."

"Ah, the year thing."

He nodded. "That's why I wanted you to have a year on your own before we got married. You needed that time to separate who you were with John, so you could learn how to be someone new—with yourself and with me."

"Do you feel like I belong to you now?"

"Most of the time. I have a feeling John and Debbi will pop up when we least expect them."

"So how do we handle that when it happens?"

"I don't know. We'll work something out." That has become Ed's go-to phrase when our life is a bit muddy.

I'm not sure we ever "worked something out." We did get to a place where it was easy to talk about John and Debbi to the boys. Using their terminology, one of us would say, "Your Old Mom or Old Dad liked to do that," or, "I remember a story about your Old Mom or Old Dad."

The toughest thing for me is the dreams. If you're awake, you can stop thoughts from taking you down paths you do not wish to travel. Dreaming is different. In the beginning of our marriage, I would dream about John when things were not going well. In my dreams, of course, our life together was always perfect. I would be shocked that he was alive and unsure what to do about Ed. We were married! How could I leave him and go with John?

John would tell me it was fine; he and Ed agreed it would be best for me to go back to my original marriage. Which of course made me mad at Ed. The next morning I would be grumpy and argumentative because he was so ready to throw away our marriage.

Then there are the Debbi dreams. I really don't like those. Even after twenty years of marriage, I still have them occasionally. The Debbi dreams involve Debbi coming back and saying she really wasn't dead. She had been in treatment and didn't want Ed to put his life on hold while she healed. Now she was better, and she wanted Ed and Andy back.

Did I mention that in these dreams, Debbi never ages? She looks amazing, and I know I can't compete with her beautiful, smooth skin and toned body. I never fight for Ed. I always let her have him because she has the rights to him, and I don't. She did have him first. I leave the house with my belongings, feeling sorry for myself that I have lost my best friend and husband. In the morning, I'm mad at Ed because he doesn't pick me—ever. He can't win after these dreams.

Now all I have to say is, "Ed, I had a Debbi dream," and he'll hug me and assure me that I am his wife, and he isn't going anywhere. He tells me to put my imagination away and look at reality. Debbi and John are in heaven; we'll see them again when we join them there, and everything will be fine. It will all work out.

And it has worked out, even though Debbi and John still pop in once in awhile. The other day, we were driving around looking at property, and we were talking. A song came on the radio that we hadn't heard in a while. It reminded Ed of something he and Debbi had done together. Right after that song, another followed—again one we hadn't heard in a while. This time it was a song that had meaning for John and me.

"I think they are in heaven celebrating that we got together. What do you think, Ed?"

"I think so too." He smiled, grasped my hand in his, and switched the radio station.

"Set me as a seal upon your heart." (Song of Solomon 8:6)

I remember an interview given by Princess Diana that caused quite a stir when it first aired. It was the first time the princess would speak publicly about the things that led to her separation and eventual divorce from her husband, Prince Charles. Reflecting on the long-term affair of the prince and his mistress, the princess of Wales remarked something to the effect, "There were three in this marriage. It was a bit crowded."

Sometimes Diana had the sensation that Debbi or John had returned. Though neither John nor Debbi had returned, and couldn't because both had died, their memories left a lasting imprint on Ed, Diana, their boys, and other family members. Sometimes it was easy to recognize and cherish thoughts and memories of the previous spouse. But at other times those thoughts of the first spouse interfered with the couple's bonding.

Has the memory of a past relationship had a negative impact on your physical, emotional, or spiritual intimacy with your spouse? Many couples come up against roadblocks to intimacy because of past relationships, lack of understanding, fear, or some other complication. How does a couple navigate around those roadblocks or avoid them altogether?

Premarital counseling can help couples avoid some of the roadblocks. If you're reading this book, however, you are likely past the premarital stage of your relationship. And let's face it—most couples will experience roadblocks to intimacy at some point along the way.

ROADBLOCKS TO PHYSICAL INTIMACY

1. Time. I have worked with many couples who state that their goal for therapy is to increase their level of physical intimacy and improve their sexual relationship. I cannot tell you how many of those same couples express that time is what holds them back: it's the wrong time of day, night, month, or there is not enough time in the day because when it comes down to it, they'd rather sleep. Or one of them would.

Author Jim Burns writes, "If you are too tired to work on your sexual intimacy then your priorities are in the wrong place." Deliberate effort must be spent tending our marital relationship, dating our spouse, talking, and having fun together. Burns recommends the following "prescription" as an antidote for couples experiencing difficulties in their intimate relationship:

1. Kiss passionately for 15 seconds every day.

2. Take 15 minutes five days a week to connect and talk.

3. Date and court your spouse at least 1.5 hours per week.

4. Schedule into your life 1.5 hours per week for sexual intimacy.[1]

Be intentional in setting apart and guarding time you will spend with your spouse. Over time, the deliberate act of scheduling, which may seem awkward at first, reinforces the importance you place on your marriage.

2. Trust. The media today often oversimplifies and misrepresents what we as Christians know about sexual union. Turn on MTV or even a major network during prime soap opera viewing time, and you will see physical relationships devoid of commitment, purely for the sake of sexual satisfaction. It gives the impression that human sexuality is simply a physical exercise, like calisthenics.

But that is not the case. Our emotions are connected to and affected by our sexual experiences. Many spouses who marry after divorce or bereavement have difficulty becoming physically intimate with another spouse because of fears and vulnerabilities. It may be difficult to trust our spouse not to hurt us or to trust ourselves to freely commit to our new spouse. Diana writes of vivid dreams in which her late husband, John, or Ed's late wife, Debbi, would appear.

A therapist might hypothesize that Diana's subconscious mind continued to process her fears regarding her marriage to Ed and might even investigate the issue of her fears that in loving Ed, she was disloyal to her first husband. Then the therapist would poke holes in that fear and engage in "reality testing."

Our sexuality is much more than just what we do beneath the sheets, and our fears can hold us back from our spouse, even though we stood at the altar and said "I do" and "I will." When dealing with remarriage following the death of a spouse, it is not unusual for the surviving spouse to feel guilty when attracted to someone other than the deceased, even when married to that person.

Following her bad dreams, Ed reminded Diana that he was there and wasn't going anywhere. Sometimes the touch of a current spouse can trigger a reaction that almost throws one back in time in a déjà vu kind of experience. If the memories are sweet, you may find that acknowledging reality may sting, but you can still savor some of that sweetness.

However, the memory can be especially disconcerting if the prior spouse was abusive, and the déjà vu experience is more akin to post trauma. If you find yourself in such a struggle, please consider seeking the help of a professional to assist with the adjustment to your new marriage and the healing of past hurts.

3. Understanding. Do you understand that God intended your sexual relationship with your husband or wife to be "an oasis of beauty for you and your spouse"?[2] Read the Song of Solomon. God created us male and female. And again, according to a later Jim Burns publication, "Since He (God) also created man and woman, He also created sexuality . . . sexuality is God's idea. Because God created our sexuality, we will want to honor Him with our bodies."[3]

Do you and your spouse understand what the Bible says about marital relationships, including sexuality? Do you understand the wonderful mechanics of your own body, how it was built to respond pleasurably to your husband or wife's intimate touch? Many adults are less informed than their children regarding physiology as it pertains to sexuality. Perhaps you are naïve about the way your body was designed, how it functions biologically. Don't be embarrassed to learn these things. You were fearfully and wonderfully made! Education about how sex works will help your marriage and assist you in providing your children the information they need at the appropriate time.

FOR MORE ABOUT ~ SEX EDUCATION RESOURCES FOR CHILDREN

Burns, Jim. *The Purity Code: God's Plan for Sex and Your Body.* Bloomington, MN: Bethany House, 2008.

Burns, Jim. *Teaching Your Children Healthy Sexuality: A Biblical Approach to Preparing Them for Life.* Bloomington, MN: Bethany House, 2008.

Learning About Sex series from Concordia Publishing House

FOR MORE ABOUT ~ MARITAL INTIMACY

Allendar, Dan, and Tremper Longman III. *Intimate Allies.* Carol Stream, IL: Tyndale House, 1999.

Burns, Jim. *Creating an Intimate Marriage: Rekindle Romance through Affection, Warmth and Encouragement.* Bloomington, MN: Bethany House, 2006.

Eyer, Richard C. *Marriage Is Like Dancing.* St. Louis: Concordia, 2007.

Gardner, Tim Allen. *Sacred Sex: A Spiritual Celebration of Oneness in Marriage.* Portland: WaterBrook Press, 2002.

Leman, Kevin. *Sex Begins in the Kitchen.* Grand Rapids: Revell Books, 2006.

Wheat, Ed, and Gaye Wheat. *Intended for Pleasure.* Grand Rapids: Revell Books, 2010.

Wilson, Barbara. *Kiss Me Again.* Portland: Multnomah, 2009.

Removing the roadblocks that obstruct the path to emotional connectedness may have a positive impact on your sexual intimacy. Marriage therapists say that the most sensitive erogenous zone is between your ears. Showing unconditional affection and love for our spouse can encourage emotional intimacy. Demonstrating respect, courtesy, and appreciation for our spouse—even when we disagree—is God pleasing. These actions also provide the proper model for our children.

Emotional transparency, willingness to share thoughts and feelings honestly, also fosters emotional intimacy, and enhances physical intimacy. A husband or wife who experienced past abuse may find emotional openness difficult, even frightening. Demonstrate you are safe by honoring your spouse's confidence. Remind your spouse that the abuser is not present. You are, and seek to honor your beloved with your heart, your mind, and your body.

SPIRITUAL INTIMACY

I'd like to offer some questions for you to ponder regarding spiritual intimacy:

- Where does God fit in your marriage? The faith foundation is needed in every aspect of your life, in all the elements of your relationship with your spouse. Fellowship with other Christians is good for you individually, as part of a couple, and as a family member.

- Is your devotional life limited to Sunday morning?

- Do you worship in your home daily with your spouse and family?

- Where is God at bedtime? Do you pray with your spouse at day's end?

- Do you thank God for your sexual relationship?

- Do you honor your spouse through your physical, emotional, and spiritual connections?

- Who is in your bedroom? Does your intimate relationship with your spouse glorify God?

"Your love is better than wine." (Song of Solomon 1:2)

11

Opening Up to the Extended Family

All would be blissful if it were only your families you had to blend. There are so many others involved besides your nuclear group. Some of your extended family will shock you with their open-arms acceptance, and others will bring you great distress because they aren't willing to embrace the changes in your life.

"So how many grandparents are we going to have?" Andy asked from the back of the van.

"Lots." I was driving through an intersection—no time for explanations.

"So we'll get more presents for our birthdays and Christmas?" That was Ben, always looking at the bottom line.

"You'll get more prayers." I glanced in the review mirror. Stunned faces looked back. At their age, presents were more tangible than prayers. "Yes, I suppose you'll get more gifts too. But prayers are more important."

⌒

Ed and I were confident that my mom and his parents would accept the new kids as their grandchildren. We were right.

Ed's parents, Oscar and Elsie, asked Ben and Josh to call them Grandma and Grandpa right away. On Fridays after school, Oscar would take all the boys down to the corner gas station for a treat, just as he had always taken Andy.

Elsie watched Josh for me several times when I went on field trips with the other two boys, even though she was running an upholstery shop out of their home. When Ed and I attended landscaping conferences, Oscar and Elsie would come and stay at our house with the children or take them into their home. Not once did they refuse to help us with the boys.

Without taking a breath, my mom accepted Andy. Right away, she said, "Come give Grandma a hug." She, too, spent time taking all the boys for a day or two. When she retired, she moved to our town to be closer. On Friday nights, she watched them for a few hours, so Ed and I could have date night. Once she bravely rode in the backseat of the van with the boys for six hours, so she could watch Andy participate in a gymnastics tournament in Chicago.

Because Debbi's mom was my aunt, I was positive she would be accepting of my boys. After all, they were related to her. She had also lost a spouse and remarried, so it seemed logical she would understand our desire to unify our little group.

However, I was concerned about John's parents. His dad hadn't been overjoyed when I married Ed, refusing to come to the wedding. I knew it was going to be difficult for John's parents to accept Ed. Their loss was still very fresh; losing a son isn't the same as losing a spouse. I understood the difference between types of grief, having lost all of my brothers. A spouse can't be replaced, but the feeling of being loved, supported, and desired by another can be. Would they be able to look past their hurt and accept Andy?

I had made a promise to John's mom when he was in the hospital awaiting surgery for the brain tumor. We were watching a talk show in the waiting room, and the topic was grandparents who aren't allowed to see their grandchildren. It was gut-wrenching to hear the devastation in those grandparents' voices; the sadness on their faces made me angry. How could anyone take the grandparents' rights away? I promised John's mom that would never happen. Even if John died and I remarried, I would always make sure she was in contact with her grandkids. Much later, she told me how much that meant to her, but at the time, she was a bit shocked when I said it. So was I because I was sure they would tell us after surgery they were able to remove the entire tumor. Maybe it was a "God moment" to reassure both of us after John died.

Ed and I brainstormed ideas on presenting a solid family unit. We were a family. We didn't want other relatives messing with the structure by singling out one child as different because he was a biological grandchild. We also felt it important that the boys maintained a relationship with their biological grandparents. It was a dilemma.

Knowing that watching all three boys at once could be a stressful event, Ed came up with what we thought would be a good plan. We would suggest to the grandparents they at least make an offer of taking each of the boys, one at a time. That way, if there was a problem of one set of grandparents accepting one or two of the boys as grandchildren, we could work around it. We would say, "Grandma asked you to come today, but we've made plans to do this fun activity as a family." We weren't sure it would work, but it was a plan.

John's parents didn't need the plan. They loved Andy and included him in everything. As a mom, I loved that at the beginning of summer, they took the boys to Table Rock Lake for a few days. What a wonderful gift to the boys and to me! Strong bonds were built on those trips with the grandparents and among the boys themselves. It also gave Ed and me a chance to spend time alone, to eat grown-up food, and to ride bikes together without screaming, "Move over! There's a car!" But by the end of those three days, I couldn't wait for them to come back home. Our house was too quiet and too clean!

The sad part of this plan is that it didn't work with Debbi's mom. She only wanted a relationship with Andy, so we chose to include her when there were family gatherings. For a while, she would give all the kids gifts at Christmas and birthdays, and then she started singling out Andy by making his special cookies and nothing for the others. Later, she would only give him gifts. He hated that. He had brothers, he loved them, and it bothered him that they weren't accepted. I wish I had known how to fix this problem. Everyone lost out in this situation. We tried to help Andy keep things quiet, so his brothers wouldn't be hurt. Ben and Josh figured it out, though, and they have no desire to have a relationship with my aunt. Andy has a minor relationship, but he's still bothered by the rejection of his brothers. Ed, however, was perfectly willing to be confrontational with his former in-laws and alienate people who were a part of his life in the past so that his new family wouldn't feel the hurt of nonacceptance.

"It took me by surprise that anyone would want to risk not having these kids be part of their life," Ed said. "So when presented with the situation, I may not have handled it the correct way."

"But to all who did receive Him, who believed in His name, He gave the right to become children of God, who were born, not of blood nor of the will of the flesh nor of the will of man, but of God." (John 1:12)

We all have situations we wish we could do over. Ed was protective of his family. He and Diana had worked so hard to promote unity among the boys that he would not tolerate the behaviors by other family members that would threaten the family's stability.

The truth is we will rarely make a decision that will please all our extended family members. Please be sensitive to the possibility that the siblings, parents, and others who were close to the previous spouse may hold great allegiance to that individual, regardless of whether the former spouse is living or dead. Relatives on the fringe of your nuclear family may have the hardest time adjusting to your family's new dynamic. That may be partly because information usually ripples out in concentric circles, those closest to us learning our important news first. Therefore, it takes longer for friends and relatives not in the "inner circle" to receive information and, thus, make adjustments. Recognize that not all of our loved ones will accept the changes our new family brings to the larger group at the same time. Be patient, and remember that humans are fallible, but God is faithful. Experts say blended families can expect some rejection, particularly early on. But don't return negative behaviors in kind. The obligation to protect the family and safeguard our children is always the first priority. How do we do this without being drawn into conflict or swept up in emotionally charged exchanges?

- Have realistic expectations: if Uncle George has always been brutally outspoken, don't expect that will change. But don't seat a sensitive spouse or child next to him at your Thanksgiving dinner.

- Model appropriate interactions: treat others as you wish you and your family to be treated.

- Respect all family members, even contentious ones.

- Use gentle assertion to set boundaries.

- Only fight *your* battles: don't let others draw your blending family into family conflicts that already exist. Sometimes family members will aggressively reach out to the newly blended family in attempts to give the appearance that you are on their side.

- Heal relationships to the best of your abilities.

- Do whatever you can to promote healthy communication between extended family and your newly blended family.

The importance of communication cannot be overstated. Survey respondent Marianne encourages families to keep communication open and talk about everything. She and her husband hold monthly family meetings in which the family talks about rules and problems and celebrate successes. Marianne and her husband plan for family fun, including a family activity, during their family meeting. Other families hold more frequent meetings, weekly or biweekly. Successful family meetings mean that parents equip their children with skills to enable healthy and effective communication.

Begin a conversation with the use of feeling statements like:

- I feel angry when . . .

- I'm happiest when . . .

- The thing I miss most is . . .

- I wish my family would/wouldn't . . .

- I know God loves me because . . .

- I feel left out when . . .

Teach your children respectful speaker/listener behaviors. These are basic common courtesies that should be employed by all family members during family meetings and in day-to-day conversation. Utilizing respectful speaker/listener behaviors provides a framework for successful discussion and encourages adults and children to enjoy peaceful exchanges of ideas and feelings.

COMMUNICATION TIPS

1. Only one person speaks at a time.

2. Do not interrupt or talk over the family member who has the floor.

3. Everyone gets a turn.

4. Listen. When it is not your turn, do not plan ahead what your next point will be. LISTEN!

5. Utilize feeling statements like, "I feel left out when you don't say good-bye when you leave for work."

6. When expressing opinions, state them as such.

7. No filibustering. Don't try to make others accept your position by wearing them out. Remember point three.

8. Don't play archaeologist. No digging up old bones. If you are working to resolve a conflict, stick to the topic at hand.

9. Eliminate all-or-nothing talk such as, "You always" or "You never," from discussions.

10. Discuss conflict in good faith with the goal of resolution.

11. Speak the truth in love.

Discussions about sensitive issues involving extended family are more challenging to navigate. Debbi's mom's behaviors, which were uncomfortable for Andy and made Josh and Ben feel left out, are not uncommon, given the circumstances. Andy is a living, breathing link to her deceased daughter. Her actions may simply have been her best effort to maintain connection and might not have demonstrated intent to exclude the other boys. It is very possible that her grief, and the facts of her daughter's illness and death, kept Andy's grandmother from recognizing the greater impact of her exclusive focus on Andy. Diana might have started a gentle discussion opening with, "You must miss Debbi so much. So do I. I'm so glad Andy knows he can count on you. I know he misses her too. Having brothers has made it easier for him. I hate to bring this up because I'm so glad he has you."

Situations like this abound in families affected by divorce, where often-hurt feelings lead to bitterness. Again, children are to be protected from hurtful behaviors. Sometimes we protect them by helping them recognize that not every situation is fair. Grandparents may take awhile to warm up to the new family situation and relatives. Reassure your children that your family's stability does not depend on the opinions of extended family members.

If your children's feelings are hurt by Grandma, Grandpa, an uncle, or an aunt, as sometimes happens, be compassionate. Tell them you are sorry they have been hurt, even if you are not the offender. Be prepared to address family members with your blended family's "policies" regarding gifts, visits, and phone calls.

Custody arrangements can result in the separation of siblings for periods of time. Children returning from visitation to the other home may return with gifts, money, and experiences all children are unable to share. Some of this is unavoidable and needs to be addressed. Honest discussions about the differences between homes can help teach children that this is a part of life.

You can avoid a certain level of conflict when by having a frank, respectful discussion with the other parent. Share your home's policies, and invite the other parent to share his or her policies. Pray that God will give you a peaceful heart at the outset of such a discussion and a peaceful outcome at the end.

> *"And the peace of God, which surpasses all understanding, will guard your hearts and your minds in Christ Jesus."* *(Philippians 4:7)*

12

Babies, Babies, Babies— or Not?

It was one of those days. All three of the angels were playing together—no arguments, just peaceful, brotherly love. A sister would have fit in so well; I just knew it. And if God wouldn't give Ed and me a little girl, another little boy would be just as perfect. I just needed to convince Ed that another baby was just what this happy home needed.

"Give it back!"

"Mom!"

I watched the tug of war for a moment. "Stop it, or you're going to your rooms!"

Okay, maybe not so angelic, but I still wanted another baby.

"Ed, I think we should procreate." I liked to use big words in front of the kids; most of the time, they ignored me, and I could converse with Ed.

Ed tipped his head toward the kids fighting over blocks. "I think we've procreated enough."

"But I always wanted to have three kids." I gave him my best "I am so sad" look.

He pointed at each bent head, "One, two, three. Done."

I pursed my lips and glared at him. "That's not what I meant. I wanted to physically have three. Four kids would be so much fun."

"I always wanted to build three houses. Can I do that? I've already built two."

"It's not the same thing, Ed." I let the subject drop—for the moment.

Every morning I would roll over and open my eyes to see "that." It was a print of a baby, a beautiful baby, the kind you want to snuggle and breathe the sweet baby smell of and touch that soft skin. The baby print resided over the top of Ed's dresser, hanging where Debbi had hung it. Ed had given it to her when Andy was born. She loved that print; I know because he told me. It was one of the things that had previously decorated our home that he wanted to keep. I get it; it's beautiful, but it made me sad, then angry—every morning. I wanted another baby, and as time went on, I was more specific in my pleas to Ed and God. I wanted a girl. I could see her little cherub face, Ed's cappuccino brown eyes, my blond hair, and a blend of the boys' personalities—their softer sides. I was feeling very left out in this house teeming with testosterone.

"Tell me again why you don't want to have a baby with me." Tears burned my eyes. "I'm a good mom."

Ed took my hands and engulfed them in his. "I never said you weren't a good mom. I want to have more time for us. There would be four years between Josh and a baby. We didn't get to have 'before kid' time together. I want us to have some 'after kids move out' time to do things, like explore the country, go to Alaska by train, or hike the Appalachian Trail. And we have three kids to put through college now; four will be impossible."

"I'm not giving up this quest."

"I know," Ed sighed. "We'll talk about it again, I'm sure."

And then one day, God answered my prayer—sort of. My brother had died before his daughter Karla was born. Cheryl, Karla's mom, was in the navy and had been assigned a temporary tour of duty in Italy for six months. There wasn't another parent to leave Karla with, and her mom wanted to leave her with family. I was family! I was getting a girl—at least for a little while.

Karla and Josh are only three months apart in age. Now it felt like we had two sets of twins, even though none of the kids were twins.

Having a girl in the house changed things a lot. No longer could I say, "Boys, it's time to go." Now I had to say, "Go get the Big Boys, Littles. It's time to go." Mom short-speak is important when there are many little ones to direct.

Then I discovered something else. This little girl had hair. And she didn't like to have it brushed. I thought all little girls liked to have their hair brushed and wear cute ribbons.

Karla added so much to our family. She fit right in, aggressive enough to hold her own in a house of boys and girly enough to win Ed's heart. I also now had someone to take shopping. I just didn't anticipate how much she would like buying! I made her a lot of girly dresses and had her picture taken for Easter with a parasol and white lace gloves. We did dress-up photos of her wearing my wedding gown. And an added bonus! We watched little girl movies together.

It was heavenly, except when it wasn't. Girls scream—loudly. They slam doors. They have moods that change faster than Ed can change channels with the remote. They want to wear your good jewelry, try your perfume, and dress the dog. They will spill nail polish on the only unstained part of the carpet. They can get your sons to do things you don't want them to. They will ruin their best outfit by climbing pine trees. They eat more slowly than boys, a lot more slowly.

I called my mom in desperation. "She's driving me insane. She talks all the time, and I can't even let her go outside alone anymore."

"Why? What happened?"

"She is so independent. I tell her to stay close, and she thinks walking a quarter mile away to the neighbor's lake and feeding the ducks is close! And Mom, she talks to everybody she meets— she doesn't know a stranger. That's scary."

My mom laughed. "Sounds like you when you were little. So how do you like having an almost-daughter?"

"I'm sorry, Mom, that I did that to you. I love having her though." And I did. I learned a lot from having Karla stay with us. Always put tights on a little girl because they don't sit like little ladies when they go up for the children's sermon. If there is a full bottle of scented hand soap when they go into a bathroom, it is likely to be empty when they leave. And little girls love you like little boys can't. They notice when you are sad and give you a hug without asking. I was sad to see her go back home to her mom. I cried for a long time.

Ed and I never did have more kids, even though the discussion continued. We both felt having Karla completed our family, but there was no way we could find someone to take her place. Having a baby would have been completely different. Sometimes I'm still sad that we didn't, but then I thank God for giving me a small taste of having a daughter. Now He's blessing me with daughters-in-law, and that's perfect.

"Rejoice in the Lord always." (*Philippians 4:4*)

The prospect of adding another child, one who is connected through DNA to both parents, is a point of tension for some couples, a source of excitement for others, and for still others it is a moot point. Diana's heart ached for a fourth child, a child that would bond her blended family. Ed presented some practical considerations. Some of his concerns would impact the whole family, and others would affect only the couple. A couple discussing adding another child to their blended family should consider the following:

- Is your family on solid ground? We have all heard of situations in which a baby is conceived in hopes that the child will strengthen a marriage that is on shaky ground. It rarely does. Similarly, if there is turmoil among your children, is a baby expected to act as a ballast? It may do the opposite. Consider some family or pastoral counseling sessions to help you and your family, pre- or post-baby.

- Are you bonded to the children you have brought to your blended family? How strong would your children say your connection is to each of them?

DO YOU KNOW ME?

Parent/Child Discussion Starters

1. Who is your child's best friend?

2. What is his or her biggest fear?

3. How can you tell your child is anxious or scared?

4. What was his or her proudest moment?

5. To whom does your child turn for encouragement?

6. How does your child know God loves him or her?

7. How does your child know that you love him or her?

- Do you and your spouse have the time to commit to an infant and to your other children too? Developing good organization practices enables us to do more with the finite number of hours in the day. Most large families that function well rely strongly on effective organization. A well-organized home can also help relieve stress caused from poorly managed schedules and mismanaged use of important resources, such as time and money.

- Are your finances in order? Can you afford another child? I think we've all heard people say, "If we waited until we could afford to have a baby, we would never have had one." If you and your spouse are already fighting about money, seek some good guidance regarding finances. Money, or lack of it, may not be a determining factor, but proper use of money is a very important consideration.

Should you and your spouse be surprised by an unplanned pregnancy and financially unprepared, look at places to trim your family's expenditures. Check the Internet for coupons and rebates. There are several sites that will alert you to good deals. Cut back on the purchase of nonessential items, and model for your children that this is an expected behavior. Do you need cable service with 300 channels or GPS on your cell phone and in your car? God surprises us with many blessings. Sometimes those blessings come with wiggling toes and feet.

It may be true that few of us can afford children from a strictly financial perspective, but that should not preclude us from using wisdom in practical matters like finances. And how do you define *affordability*? Having in savings enough cash to pay for everything a child needs, from diapers to college tuition? Having a savings protocol in place, so you have funds available for a wedding when the time comes? Or having the amount of money required to pay this month's bills, and you'll worry about the next round when you tear the current calendar page away?

- Do you have the space, or can you make the space?
  Survey respondent Marianne listed space boundaries among one of her family's challenges and priorities. This echoes priorities voiced by family life experts. Personal space is important. Consider age differences and developmental stages when determining how to assign bedrooms. A twelve-year-old girl experiencing all the changes that go with puberty, including menstruation and physical development, should not be required to share a room with a four-year-old brother. Consider arranging your home so the new baby and the four-year-old become roommates. Permitting the four-year-old to help choose decorating elements that are agreeable to you both, such as paint color or theme, may give that child a sense of belonging and ownership and smooth the transition.

The determination to conceive a child is between a husband, a wife, and God, but sometimes God gives gifts that surprise us, maybe even shock us. I was beyond shocked—I was horrified—to learn I was unexpectedly pregnant with my fourth child. My older children, ages fifteen, thirteen and ten, were horrified too. My oldest walked around muttering "Idiots!" under his breath for two days. Then he and I were in a very serious car accident, totaling our van. His first question as the steam rose from our engine was, "Mom, are you okay?" I thought I was, but the air bag had gone off, and I didn't know how the impact would affect the baby. And as you might guess, considering the ages of my children, I was not a young mom.

"Erik," I said, "if this little baby is okay, then God really wants her in our family." She was. At her birth, I marveled that God knew we needed her.

Kristen, the baby, has been the magnet drawing our family together at a time when older kids are striking off on their own. At high school functions, Erik would carry her through the halls. He had discovered Kristen's potential as "chick bait." Heidi, my older daughter, finally has a sister. Kristen is a little sister who eagerly counts the hours until Heidi's return, hairbrush and nail polish at the ready. And Travis is a tender, protective big brother and an awesome babysitter. He takes Kristen along when he goes out to eat and to movies with his buddies. Kristen returned from a recent outing with the news that Travis and his friends—surrogate big brothers Dann, Austin, and Richter—had established an alliance and promised to use their impressive karate skills on any boy who asks her out when she reaches dating age.

When we learned we were expecting that fourth child, many adjustments were necessary. An infant requires a different level of child care than ten, thirteen, and fifteen-year-olds. Living space was redesigned, our budget reevaluated, and daily schedules overhauled.

But just as God blessed us with an unexpected gift, he knew we needed Kristen in our family. He blessed and strengthened us through all the changes and adjustments. You may welcome a baby into your blended family. Or like Ed and Diana, you may enjoy the procreating success you have already achieved. No matter the number of people in our household, God is faithful and provides all that we need during the easy times and during the times of adversity.

> "But grace was given to each one of us according to the measure of Christ's gift." (Ephesians 4:7)

13

Crime and Punishment
Is Not a Family Game

What do you get when you mix a zero-tolerance parent with a "let's talk about this" parent? Chaos. And lots of it. What do you get if those parents flip that role repeatedly? Double chaos and confused kids.

Because of their cancer, both of our previous spouses had uncontrollable anger problems. Debbi's leukemia and John's brain tumor caused them both great emotional grief and sometimes the inability to control their emotions. John's anger left me afraid and ready to protect Ben and Josh. Debbi's anger had the same effect on Ed. That left us in Shaky Discipline Land. Neither of us wanted to come on so strongly that we alienated the boys, driving them further in the wrong direction.

Ed was always willing to discuss problem behaviors with the kids, while I wanted to punish them with a time-out or an unpleasant chore. It was seldom that we agreed, and often we did not back up the other's decision. Yet somehow it worked—most of the time. We never disagreed with the choice the other made in front of the kids. One of the hardest things to do was to let go of how we had planned to raise the boys with the previous spouse.

One of our first lessons in our differences occurred when we discovered Ben had helped himself to Andy's stash of change. Andy had stored away quite a bit of change from his Friday afternoon trips to the store with his grandfather.

Oscar and Elsie had been on a trip, and as souvenirs they bought the boys busses that were banks. Andy, excited to put his change in his, ran to his room with his bus and loaded it almost to the top.

Ben and Josh didn't have any change. Ed gave them a few quarters to put in their busses. The wheels on the busses rolled, so the boys turned the living room into a freeway with bus stations and tours to the mountains. Tired, they put the busses back in their rooms.

Then Saturday came.

"I've been robbed! We have to call the police!" Andy held his bank over his head as he ran into the room.

Sure enough, his once heavy bus was now on the light side. We questioned Ben and Josh. No, they didn't know where Andy's money went. Ben had one of those "I know something" looks that guilty kids wear.

"Ben, do you know where Andy's money went?" Ed asked.

Eventually, he confessed. "It's not fair. I don't have as much as Andy."

We made him give it back and apologize. I excused his behavior to Ed. "He really doesn't have the same things. Most of his toys are still at the house in Missouri."

I knew more drastic measures needed to be taken. This wasn't behavior we could ignore. Still, knowing how John would have reacted if he were alive scared me. The brain tumor had triggered violent anger, and he would react without thinking. John would have spanked Ben and sent him to his room for hours. How would Ed react to Ben's thievery?

Ed realized that for me this was traumatic and one of those moments that could define our marriage. He decided to give Ben the honesty talk instead of punishment.

Josh never seemed to be in trouble. Could it be he was observant and learned from his brothers' troubles? Possibly, or so I thought, despite the other two telling me that Josh started something that seemed beyond his years and capabilities, being five years younger. Then one summer after defending him in the pool for years, I discovered something about the baby of the family. He caused trouble when he thought he wasn't being seen. When I looked up, he was on Andy's back, trying to dunk him in the water. The very thing I forbade them to do to him! Shocking, I know. Who would have thought the baby of the family would get away with anything?

Andy seemed to be the child who created the most chaos. Ben and Josh, when disciplined with just words, would shrink in size and tear up; they knew they had done something wrong and disappointed us.

Andy preferred to argue and redirect any blame from himself. We thought he might decide on the law as a career. I wasn't capable of keeping up with his fast-flying redirects. He seemed to know that. In seconds, he could have my voice screeching and my face flushed. I agonized over this. How could I, who had been a teacher and fairly successful at disciplining two other children, fail so much with Andy?

Ed said Andy and I were too much alike. We conflicted on everything every day. Our very first argument came when, at eight years old, he refused to tie his own shoes. His dad always tied them, and Andy saw no need to do it. He knew how; he just didn't want to. The first week of school, he carried his shoes to the car, saying he wouldn't put them on and tie them.

The trip to school was a stressful argument match instead of a calming, joyful time. We would get to school, and Ben would get out of the car. Andy would hold up the car line while putting on his shoes and then tying them himself. By the next week, he was ready on time. Ed felt I should relent on this. It was something I could do in seconds, so why fight over it? Did I mention that Ed didn't have to get the three of them dressed, get the correct book bags and lunch boxes in their hands, and drive them to school?

As the teenage years arrived, the stress tripled. Andy and a friend were caught smoking in his bedroom. Ben bought a truck we didn't know about. And Josh? We're still waiting for that story to be told. We had our trips to the police station, and community service had to be served. I wanted to move where no one knew our name. Ed kept telling me they were not bad kids and that it would all work out.

Discipline became the tiger in our marriage. If there was an undesirable action, I wanted a reaction that would have the kids rethinking ever doing that activity again. I wanted the boys to be like all the other kids in our church family—perfect. It wasn't until after the kids were on their own that I discovered the parents I admired most had the same difficulties we had—and they weren't in a blended marriage! One mom told me she struggled with making her family look good all the time and had to deal with the pressure of other moms resenting her for it. How I wish I had known we were normal.

"Train up a child in the way he should go; even when he is old he will not depart from it." (Proverbs 22:6)

Discipline is a tiger in many marriages and an obstacle for most couples. We set ourselves up for disappointment when we expect perfection. Our Lord was the only human who could claim perfection. We frustrate and confuse our children when we can't agree on appropriate behavioral guidelines and discipline practices (more on collaborative parenting and discipline in the next chapter). As Diana realized, normal families are imperfect.

Imperfect moms and dads are entrusted with the care of their sons and daughters. Not just feeding and clothing them, but teaching them the things of God. We teach and demonstrate God's love through our behavior and the example set by our day-to-day family interactions. The manner in which a man responds to his wife provides his sons a living example to follow, one that is often passed from generation to generation. A husband's interactions with his wife also instruct his daughters on what to expect from their husbands. A woman teaches her children in similar fashion: the old adage "more is caught than taught" certainly is born out as family behavior patterns pass from one generation to the next. How humbling to consider the consequences of a parent's behavior on future generations: the truth that how I speak to and behave toward my husband is a model for both my sons and daughters.

The discipline tools we bring to our marriages include what we learn from our families of origin plus, in Ed and Diana's case, experiences from an earlier marriage. The most important discipline tool, however, is the instruction given by God in His Holy Word. Turning from behavior that is not God pleasing may be difficult, especially when that behavior was the rule of thumb in our families of origin or an earlier marriage, but it is important for the health of our nuclear families.

God has set guidelines, or boundaries, in place. Henry Cloud and John Townsend define a boundary as "a property line that defines a person; it defines where one person ends and someone else begins."[1] God also uses boundaries to instruct us regarding the behavior He desires from His children and the behavior He forbids. While Ed and Diana were still in the process of developing a shared approach to discipline, the boys clearly understood that some behaviors were acceptable, and others were not. Though they were young, the boys also understood that broken rules resulted in consequences—perhaps even notifying the police!

KAREN

"Discipline was a very difficult problem in trying to merge the two families. My husband would rant and rave about the girls being out later than they were supposed to be, and then greet them with hugs and kisses when they did get home. His son could do no wrong and, I felt, was harmed by overprotection. My adopted son was always on the outside. My husband gave him his name but never once told him 'I love you.' Our only disagreements were over what we considered best for the children. It was probably a daily problem with one or the other."

Survey Says . . .

Most of our survey respondents indicated that they did not use corporal punishment, but utilized time-outs, restrictions, and loss of privileges instead. There was a unison response regarding the importance that parents consider a child's developmental stage, match punishment to the offense, and present a united front when responding to the misdeeds of their youngsters. Terry wrote of the strain discipline can place on a couple's relationship:

We had family councils and made decisions about rules, curfews, chores, and allowances. We then attached penalties appropriate to the infraction.

In the beginning, my husband, Noel, and I determined that it was important to put money in the bank before trying to make a withdrawal. So we each continued to handle discipline for our own children while staying within the framework that had been determined by the family councils. Since I was home all the time, and Noel worked long hours, it became necessary for me to begin enforcing rules after a couple of months. This was met with resistance, even though Noel backed up my decisions when he got home. Sometimes our children would stand together against us. There were times when Noel and I would go up into our bedroom, shut the door, and just stand there and hold each other, praying for comfort because it really felt like them against us.

Louise, whose husband had two children by a previous marriage, spoke to a common difficulty among families with whom the children do not have permanent residency, but rather visitation arrangements. Louise said, "There was little discipline going on, especially at first. My husband wanted his time with the kids to be fun." Louise shared that this was a prescription for disaster. Her advice? "Know your values, your limits, and stick to your guns!"

Terry and Noel, Louise, and almost all our other survey respondents spoke emphatically of the importance that parents bring the cares of their hearts to God in prayer and stand united as husband and wife in the face of parenting struggles.

Boundaries

Another thing Ed and Diana had going for them was the fact that each supported the other's discipline choice in the presence of their boys. An invisible boundary also surrounded the parental unit, appropriately setting the parents and adult concerns apart from those of the children. Discipline disagreements were held behind closed doors. A boundary was in place that separated the parents from the children in matters of discipline. Not all disagreements need be held privately. We can teach our children to respectfully disagree and resolve conflict in healthy ways. But as we will read in the next chapter, parental unity is a vital component of effective discipline.

Discipline has several components. Teaching, modeling, and guiding are a part of the discipline wheel, along with correction and consequences.

Discipline Wheel

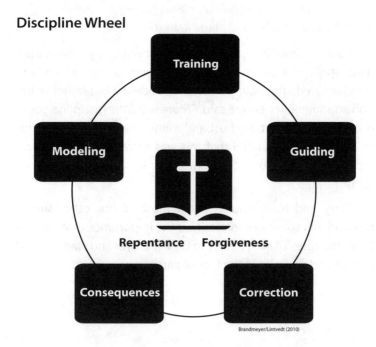

Brandmeyer/Lintvedt (2010)

Having an intimate knowledge of each child as a unique creation compels parents to assess situations requiring intervention individually. Diana was aware of the different ways her sons responded to discipline. In attempts to guide each child in a manner that will teach that child most effectively, the administration of guidance (discipline) may not look identical in all circumstances. The loss of privileges may swiftly curb one child's misbehavior, but another child may make a behavior change in response to a stern word from a parent. Yet another may require correction and consequence time and again before behavior is modified.

Discipline practices are complicated when a child has more than one household and set of parents. In the best of all worlds, agreement and consistency would exist in all corners of a child's environment. This is not always the case. Consistency within your home, at least, is imperative.

Many therapists and child care experts say that a parent's goal is to teach responsibility in the context of faith.[2] The heart of discipline is teaching responsibility, curbing misbehavior, and applying consequence to transgression.

The amazing blessing that Christian households enjoy is grace. Moms and dads are held in a grip of grace. We have the opportunity to model in our homes, to the best of our feeble abilities, God's grace. It may be in the form of a talk rather than a spanking. It may be in the manner we demonstrate for our children that they start with a clean slate, that forgiveness is complete because Christ's blood has covered all our sins. God loves moms and dads through our brokenness, and empowers us to love our children through good behavior and bad.

> *"Be kind to one another, tenderhearted, forgiving one another, as God in Christ forgave you." (Ephesians 4:32)*

14

Divide and Conquer: Whose Side Are You On?

The Olympics may have their super-strength games with well-trained athletes, but my kids are gold medal winners in the "But Mom Said, But Dad Said" games.

I came out of our bedroom and passed the bathroom the boys shared. It was Andy's turn to brush his teeth in the bathroom. I walked past the open door. I did a robot blink, stopped, and backed up two steps.

Andy was brushing his teeth while standing on top of the carnation pink counter in sock feet. He appeared to be skating while brushing.

"What are you doing?" I could feel my jaw clench.

"Brushing." He spat in the sink from what seemed to be ceiling height.

"Get down, now."

"Dad lets me brush my teeth this way." He continued to skate. The gauntlet had been tossed. And there was only going to be one winner.

"Get. Down. Now. There's a new rule in this house. There will be no standing on any counters in this house ever."

Andy sprang off the counter. "I'm calling Dad. He'll tell you."

And the game began.

"You can't call him; he's working." The small whirlwind spun. I grabbed and caught just the edge of his sleeve. My fingers lost traction, and he left my fingers waving in the air. He galloped down the stairs. I was right behind him. His hand shot out and snagged the phone, and his finger punched in the number before I could stop him.

"Dad! Mom's mad at me. She won't let me stand on the counter. Tell her you let me." Andy's face was flushed.

I couldn't hear what Ed was saying. "Let me talk to your father."

Andy smirked and held the phone out to me. "Dad wants to talk to you."

I snatched it from him. Ed had told Andy they would talk about it when he got home. And yes, he had always let Andy stand on the counter to brush his teeth. They had started that when he was little, so he could see in the mirror. Would I mind waiting until he got home to discuss it? He would then talk to Andy about the need to make some changes.

We repeated this pattern in various ways. Sometimes, Andy and I would race to the door to get to Ed in the evening. I was fighting for the authority and power. And so was Andy.

Ed had his own troubles disciplining Ben and Josh. While they didn't play the "mom said" card, they had their own method of creating doubt.

Ed was used to Andy's argument process. Ed dubbed it the "throw out any statement to see if you can get the parent to forget the trouble you're in" method. He would keep going back to the issue that had caused Andy to be in a sticky situation. I never developed this highly desired skill. My arguments with Andy would spiral into many dimensions at warp speed.

When Ed needed to discipline Ben or Josh, he would gear his mind for a mental battle, only to find them tearing up at the first word of reproof—every time.

Shouts every parent dreads were coming from the backseat, ricocheting off my headrest, and attaching themselves to the ends of my nerves, stretching them to a point where they might not recover. You know the ones: "Stop touching me! Don't hit my arm! You're stupid!" We had been visiting grandparents in Missouri, and the last five minutes of the trip had expanded to a decade.

I kept turning around at first, asking them to stop, then yelling at them to stop, then praying I would suddenly go deaf, as it had appeared Ed had. How could he just sit there and listen to this? I wanted to reach over and punch him in the arm, despite how it would look to the beasts in the backseat.

"Ed, do something," I hissed. Just like a snake, those words slithered between my lips, full of poison and ready to attack if he didn't do anything.

He looked at me with no expression. "We're almost home." Now I knew for sure the man I married wasn't real. He wasn't from this planet. He didn't have nerves that were frayed and twisted.

I huffed, yelled into the backseat a few more times, and clenched my nails into the palms of my hands. I could not wait to get those boys out of the backseat and show them some motherly love.

The car slid to a stop, and I let the seat belt fly, yanking open the door. Ed reached over and grabbed my arm. "Go in the house, and take Josh with you."

"Why?"

"I'm going to deal with those two. Just go inside." If you could button lips, mine would have had a row of those tiny pearl ones running across them. He was going to take care of this mess. Why he didn't do it fifty miles ago I wasn't sure, but at least now those two would understand the wrath of a parent. I pried Josh out of his car seat, and we went inside, sort of. I waited to hear the beginning of the "when your mother tells you to do something, you do it" speech. Only he wasn't saying that!

"I want the two of you in the driveway. Then you're going to box each other, without gloves, until one of you wins."

"Ed!"

"Go inside. Right now. I know what I'm doing."

Did he? Did he really? I didn't like this plan at all, but for some reason, I went inside like he said, muttering all the way upstairs with Josh. What kind of man tells his kids to hit each other? I grew angrier and angrier as I followed Josh upstairs.

At the top of the stairs, I decided no one was going to hit anyone. Wasn't that the problem in the backseat? Touching and punching? Wasn't he giving them permission to do the very thing I asked them not to do?

I went down one step when I heard two boys running for the steps. Both were crying. I was at a loss. What should I do? Who should I comfort first?

Ed stood at the bottom of the steps. "In your rooms, both of you."

I came down the stairs ready to battle this ogre who encouraged fighting. "Why did you do that? Are they hurt?"

"Only their pride. They both took one punch and found out it hurt when they got hit back. That was the end of it. They won't be hitting each other anymore. They've discovered that neither one of them is really stronger than the other. That's a good thing."

I glared at him and stomped back up the stairs to give Josh a bath, and maybe I would check on the other two.

"Don't go in their rooms. I'll talk to them in a little while."

"They better not have black eyes. We have church tomorrow."

"And though a man might prevail against one who is alone, two will withstand him—a threefold cord is not quickly broken." (Ecclesiastes 4:12)

In my business, professional mental health counseling, some might refer to Ed's approach to the problem between Ben and Andy as a "paradoxical intervention." A classic example of a paradoxical intervention is prescribing the symptom: instructing two boys who have been poking and prodding one another for a hundred miles to continue that annoying behavior and box it out.

An interesting outcome of utilizing the paradoxical intervention is that typically, a spontaneous remission of the problem or behavior is likely to occur. As was the case here, the boys could not or would not sustain their aggressive behavior once it became a mandate. Whatever purpose it had served in the backseat (distraction, test of wills/skills, unity against mom, dividing and conquering the parental alliance, or fighting boredom) dissolved in the dirt of the driveway.

Now, I must provide a disclaimer that I am *not* recommending families utilize this technique without the guidance of a trained mental health professional.

The paradoxical intervention is more likely employed with sleep problems or minor anxieties, not so much with aggressive behaviors, particularly with juveniles. Liability may be one factor that discourages professionals from utilizing paradoxical interventions to curb aggressive behaviors as Ed did. Those of us who know Ed recognize he has some natural counseling instincts and the ability to remain a calm, non-anxious presence in the face of conflict. I suspect Diana's fears, which grew as she mounted the stairs, stemmed not from the fact that Ed's unorthodox approach was his instinctual response, but that it triggered memories of John's lack of restraint as his cancer progressed. Diana demonstrated an outward trust in her husband, but she privately questioned his intervention technique.

TERRY

"We felt that the only way to treat each of our children equally was to treat each of them as an individual. We refused to allow them to pull us into a split family competition situation. We consistently maintained that we were an 'us,' and that was all there was to it. Noel and I maintained that as long as they lived in our home, they would treat each other as brother and sister and us as mom and dad, that they would obey the house rules and be respectful of all who lived there. As you can imagine, we had varied success with this, as any family would."

As she wrote earlier, while Diana and Ed had very different approaches to discipline, each spouse supported the other when he or she was disciplining one of their sons. They knew that teaching their sons the things of God, including responsibility, appropriate behavior, and self-regulation, was critical to the boys' development and the health of the family. Wading through the muddy waters of how they had parented before blending families challenged each spouse.

Author Maxine Marsolini's blended family included her two children and her husband's three. Marsolini describes how the reality of discipline impacted her and her new husband:

> Almost immediately discipline was a problem. This quickly became one of the "biggies" in our house. It affected all of us, not just the children. We could not parent effectively unless we could bring a halt to the division surrounding this subject. Only in unity would we be able to develop and administer a strategy capable of guiding our children into lifelong, socially acceptable

behavior. Somehow we had to go beyond the familiar do-what-I-say patterns of the past.[1]

Scripture has much to say on the importance of wise teaching and the truth that proper discipline is guided by love. "My son, do not despise the LORD's discipline or be weary of his reproof, for the LORD reproves him whom He loves, as a father the son in whom he delights" (Proverbs 3:11–12). God disciplines *all* those He loves. Yes, we are given boundaries, laws, and rules. And we are blessed by the Gospel of God's grace and redemption through Christ. Parents have the incredible opportunity to show the face of God to their daughters and sons as they nurture, teach, and guide them.

Perhaps parents want to pretend that God's discipline and instruction apply only to children, but that is not so. He molds us, adults and children, and shapes us into His design. Proverbs 23:12–13 reads, "Apply your heart to instruction and your ear to words of knowledge. Do not withhold discipline from a child." Our hearts are to be tender to God's teachings and wisdom and our eyes open to His counsel.

We know that, when discipline is concerned, it is not necessary that two children collaborate to drive a wedge between mom and dad. One little child on the bathroom counter, in the swimming pool, or in the playroom with his brother's bank can manage this disruption just fine, especially when parents are operating as "single threads." But when we, dads and moms, present to our families "a cord of three strands" with Christ the primary strand—the core—our instruction and discipline gain strength.

Because their boys' other biological parents had died, Ed and Diana did not face the dilemma of many blended families: negotiating the added challenge that comes when there are more than two living parents. Each had chosen to adopt the child or children of the other, so Ed and Diana as a couple were legally the parents of all three boys. Ed and Diana were united as a couple and as parents. Each worked to build a relationship with the other's son or sons. From the outset, each modeled trust and respect for the other parent, even when applying discipline, and encouraged the forming of a parent-child relationship between the nonbiologically related parent and child.

Building a relationship with stepchildren is a crucial precursor to discipline. Marsolini reminds us that discipline "is an act of love, not an opportunity to vent frustration. . . . Discipline should bring order to a child's life, not confusion."[2] Determining how all parents might unite to provide that order, while difficult at times, is not an impossible task but one that provides great blessing and enhances the social and spiritual development of children.

"Teach me, O LORD." (Psalm 119:33)

15

Dining Room or Mess Hall?

For a year, I had been serving hot dogs, pizza, and mac and cheese with an occasional green bean. I didn't feel like cooking for two small boys who wouldn't eat unprocessed food. Now that Ed and I were married, it was time for a change. Ed needed good food, and so did the boys. It was time to step up my game in the kitchen.

My first foray into the kitchen was at the Missouri house. It was a familiar place, and cooking in my kitchen shouldn't have been too traumatic. Except I had decided to start with what used to be a traditional Saturday breakfast—French toast. Memories hit with each cracked egg. I had not made this meal since John had died. I wanted it to become a special meal for my new family. I kept my emotions hidden behind a cheery mom smile, slid the toast on a plate, and set it on the table in front of my hungry males.

Andy poked the toast with his fork. "It looks weird, Dad. Do I have to eat it?"

That's all it took; tears salted my face. "Don't eat it." I turned and fled to my bedroom, where I landed like a drama queen and wailed.

In seconds, Ed was upstairs with me. Between sobs, I told him why I was crying. I soon realized the silliness of my behavior, tucked the drama queen away for another day, and went back downstairs to the kitchen. It was empty. The boys had eaten the French toast, and the only things left were the plates swimming in syrup. I could hear the boys playing in the living room.

Andy ran into the kitchen. "Mom, that was good. Can we have it next time we come here?"

I hugged him and said, "We can have it at your house too."

As a mom, I hoped to teach my children table manners that would come to them with ease as they grew into adults. Dinnertime was my chosen hour to work on these skills. Ed was tired from working, so I didn't involve him in this endeavor. I hoped he would follow along in quiet support.

I didn't know chili would be my biggest opponent.

Fixing food for five people isn't a skill God gave me. He gave me a fast finger to dial the pizza delivery guy. We had had too many pizzas that first month. Now the weather was getting cooler, and I thought chili would be a good choice. It was tomato based like pizza, you only needed one utensil to eat it, and there would be leftovers. And a bonus would be fewer dishes for the cook (me) to clean.

We said the dinner prayer, placed our napkins on our laps, and the chili, ladled in bowls, sat in front of my family.

"I hate chili." Ben nudged the bowl away from him. "There's chunks in there."

Knowing that Ed liked pieces of tomato rather than sauce, I had made it different from the kind I used to make.

"I don't want any." Andy put his napkin on the table.

I had forgotten about Ed making only chili for two years. Andy had told me he didn't ever want to eat chili again. Ever.

Josh mimicked his brother's actions. "I see an onion!"

What could I do? Should I make something else? Maybe they would eat cereal?

Ed cleared his throat, and all faces turned in his direction. "Everyone is eating chili, this chili—tonight. Your mom worked hard on providing you a nice, warm meal on a cold day. So put your napkins on your lap and eat."

Ben wanted to please his dad. He took one bite and gagged.

Andy dropped his spoon on the table, engaged by this new turn of events he hadn't witnessed in a family setting.

The rest of us watched as Ben tried to eat another bite and again gagged.

Ed put his clenched fists on the table. "Ben, eat the chili; swallow it. There is nothing in there that will hurt you."

Ben tried again and gagged.

"If you throw up that chili, I will make you eat it. It's just chili."

Ben ate the chili. Andy ate the chili. Josh ate the chili. Dinner proceeded with no conversation, and no one asked for seconds.

Ben's favorite food is now chili with chunks of vegetables.

I struggled to find a meal that everyone would eat and love. I hoped to become one of those moms whose children would request a favorite meal. There were requests. Ben and Josh wanted a dish John's mom used to make—macaroni and Swiss cheese with ham. Andy and Ed didn't like that meal. Andy wanted steaks; those didn't turn out to be edible when I made them.

I discovered a book called *Once-a-Month Cooking* by Mary Beth Lagerborg and Mimi Wilson. I shopped for hours on one day and cooked for hours the next. It was a successful plan, and it seemed the food lasted more than a month, but it wasn't a plan I wanted to continue. For me, it took away the adventure of cooking.

I tried theme dinners: Italian, Mexican, and then there was the night I tried Thai. I looked over the recipe. It called for chicken and peanut butter—two favorite ingredients. This dinner should be a hit. It was different enough to appeal to Andy and had some comfort food for Josh. Ben wasn't home that night, so I didn't have to worry about him gagging at the table.

I plated that meal like a gourmet chef had made it. After one bite, even I knew this dish was not a winner. Andy's friend, who had been invited to dinner, tried to be polite. "I like peanut butter, but not on chicken."

That was the evening a new rule was born. The "you have to try it, and if you don't like it, you can make your own dinner" rule. There was always a jar of peanut butter and bread for them to make a sandwich.

I didn't give up my search for that perfect meal. I made so many different things that no one in my family can say they like one meal more than another. They all say, "Mom, you never made the same thing twice, even if we said we liked it." Whoops. Guess I missed the overwhelming praise they offered for some of those meals.

The kitchen is an important gathering place for any family. For us, it was the room where most conversations were sprinkled with Andy demanding Josh not make noises when he ate, while his own mouth was full of food; me asking Ben to slow down when eating French fries; and all of us watching Josh cut his pancakes to the size of peas before pouring a lake of syrup. Ed or I said, "Use your napkin," countless times during each meal, and we asked each child individually, "What happened at school today?" or, "Tell us one good thing that happened today."

One day Ed had the kids move over one chair to the right. He thought they were getting too comfortable. They were upset and not just for the one night. For a week, they complained that they weren't in their chair. Ed relented and let them go back to their place at the table. Today when they come home for dinner, they want to sit in their chair. Even my daughter-in-law Sara knows not to sit in Ben's chair! We have a round, wooden table that has scratches, paint streaks, and newspaper print embedded in places. I love that table. My family was born there.

"You prepare a table before me." (Psalm 23:5)

Diana recognized the dinner table could provide an important connecting link for her family and ease the transition from two families to one. Though her memories of mealtimes spent with Ben and Josh's dad, John, were tender, Diana utilized family mealtime as the vehicle to create structure and stability for her new family. Her family's mealtime prayers helped them establish an important shared ritual. Saying grace also modeled for their boys the value Ed and Diana placed on faith, gratitude, and daily communication with God. Diana exercised her adventurous spirit, trying out new recipes that the family might adopt as their own. She was flexible enough to throw out those that didn't work well.

A basic reason to set family mealtime as a goal is the fact that family meals are associated with better nutrition, better behavior, and healthier children. The nutritional benefits are dramatic. Research indicates that children who eat more family meals are more likely to eat fruits, vegetables, and grains, and are less likely to snack on unhealthy foods. Youth who regularly have family meals also demonstrate improved school performance and concentration, in addition to less depression and substance abuse. Parents who plan a week's worth of meals to be eaten at home ahead of time see financial benefits as well.

Leanne Ely comments that the family dinner is "a place of communion, fellowship, and a means of reconnecting with those we care about most. Over simple meals important stuff happens."[1]

Over simple meals, important lessons are learned. Diana had her radar tuned to detect the teachable moments that exist in ordinary days and regular meals. She knew that during the family meal, she could teach and demonstrate important social lessons, dining behaviors, and listening skills. She tended to her family's need for nourishment and created a mealtime structure that fed her husband and boys physically, spiritually, and relationally. The boys were encouraged in their development as individuals by receiving permission to dislike certain foods. Ed and Diana wisely determined that the boys must try new foods before deciding whether or not they liked them. Placing the responsibility to make themselves a replacement meal squarely on the boys' shoulders discouraged cavalier food choices.

MARY

Mary reports that her husband and his late first wife had owned their own restaurant. Cooking was not one of Mary's specialties, and the need to provide three meals a day caused great anxiety. Her husband helped with the task, and the family enjoyed the chef's menus. Mary's menus included things her new family was not used to: Hamburger Helper meals and Chef Boyardee Pizzas doctored up with onions, mushrooms, and cheese. Though Mary says no one complained, the middle daughter decided she liked to cook and was assigned the job of the evening meal. Mary wisely handed over the supper preparations to her step-daughter and proudly shares that all benefitted from delicious meals.

Most twenty-first century families live fast-paced lives. It may seem easier to grab something from the drive-through and eat on the way to whatever event is on the family calendar, but the rewards of putting on the fast-food brakes and connecting across the dining table can be invaluable. Piles of research point out that most drive-through establishments serve food high in the things we should avoid, like sodium, cholesterol, and trans fat, and low in the good nutrients like vitamins, minerals, protein, and fiber. Less than adequate nutrition can augment stress we may face day-to-day. And a meal on the run is not good for digestion, for building healthy bodies, or for healthy relationships.

Medical doctor Alan Greene writes that each family meal can be "a calm in a sea of busyness that roils around us. It can be an oasis of connectedness and simple joy."[2]

> *"The cheerful of heart has a continual feast."*
> *(Proverbs 15:15)*

TABLE GRACE

1. Recognize God's blessings. Begin with thanksgiving.

2. Your table should be a peaceful place of respite, relationship, and community. Nourish body, mind, and soul with healthy meals and warm discussions.

3. Encourage harmony by avoiding unpleasant topics and criticism.

4. Everyone gets a turn! Involve all family members in conversation. Parents can model gracious interactions by listening well and responding respectfully.

5. Open-ended questions are good discussion starters and allow family members to express their thoughts. Questions that begin with "How . . . ", "Tell me about . . . ", "If you were the teacher/cook/ coach . . . " can get the conversation ball rolling.

6. Include children before and after serving the meal, with preparation and clean up. Not only does this encourage bonding between parent and child, but children also learn practical

skills important for the future.

7. Be joyful! Laughter is good for your health and aids digestion. Laugh with your loved ones!

●·●

Mealtime joy wasn't always on the menu when Luanne's blended family sat down for meals. She reports that mealtimes "weren't always pretty," but neither were they a catastrophe. "No one ever liked the same vegetable, so we always had a variety of vegetables for dinner. That was the only problem."

Terry's mealtime experience with her blended family of nine was a different story. She writes, "Everyone was thrilled that I was going to stay at home and not work. Both families had been single-parent households and were happy at the prospect of having a stay-at-home mom. The menus were very flexible, and since there were three large boys at the table each day, they didn't care what I served, as long as there was enough." Enough food, enough fellowship, and enough love, even for Terry's family of nine.

> *"My soul will be satisfied as with fat and rich food, and my mouth will praise You with joyful lips." (Psalm 63:5)*

16

Traditions:
You Do What on Sundays?

Owning your own business means your husband spends six days a week at the shop, every evening doing accounts and totaling deposits, and more paperwork on the seventh day. Before we were married, Ed found time to do fun things on Sunday afternoons with all of us. I wanted that time back.

When we were dating, we decided Friday nights were for us—no kids. The rest of the weekend would be about them and building family traditions. We started off well. Saturday nights, we would rent movies, pop popcorn, and huddle in front of the television. Or we would get a pizza and go to the show.

On Sunday afternoons, Ed would attach a bright yellow kid cart to the back of his bike where Josh and his army men would ride. Andy would race out of sight with Ben following and Ed or me yelling out to move over when a car was coming. The roads we biked on weren't heavily trafficked. There were tractors, dogs, and once a goat chased us!

Soon real life poked its thick fingers into our perfect plan. Paperwork overtook our summer Sundays and evenings. Then fall arrived. Ed had told me he didn't watch football. What was left unsaid was that there wasn't a team in St. Louis anymore. Then the Rams moved to town. Ed enjoyed the game, but the boys did not. That left me once again parenting single-handedly, or that's the way it felt.

I dragged out board games. Ben and Josh liked playing games. I would try to get Andy interested in playing with us. I insisted he play at least one game with us. He would turn sullen and argumentative during the game. I wanted to be fair and do something everyone would like, so I stopped playing games with them. I should have let Andy do something else and continued to play with Ben and Josh, but I wanted Andy included in this family activity.

Then Andy started gymnastics, and weekends quickly filled up with gymnastic meets. Ben took up fencing, and the rest of the weekend free time became planned time. Hours were spent on bleachers with a bag of toys and snacks for the two boys not participating. Some of those trips were fun for all of us, like when we went to Chicago with Andy for a meet and to Arkansas for the Junior Olympics to watch Ben fence.

Those activities faded, being replaced with select soccer teams for Andy. He played on two teams. Every weekend brought games to watch, some close by and others out of state. By this time, Ben and Josh weren't doing anything extra on weekends. Their activities—drum lessons and Scouts—occurred during the week.

We started leaving Ben at home to watch Josh when the games were nearby. At first, that was freeing because I didn't have to entertain them on the sidelines, and we were only gone for a few hours. After several years of doing this, it occurred to me that we were not doing things as a family. I wanted a change. I began staying home from the games to do things with Ben and Josh. I felt sad because they weren't getting any time with Ed.

Then I was asked to write a few pieces for a local family magazine. They asked me to take my family to different places in the area, take some photos, and write a story. Ed began going with us, and Andy caught rides to his games with another family.

An assignment to report on orienteering at the arboretum in Gray Summit, Missouri, happened to fall on one of Andy's game days. I begged Ed to go with me and the other two boys. I can't read a map, and had a feeling we would be lost for days if it were my responsibility to bring us back to the beginning. Ed made the tough choice to go with us, but Andy wasn't happy about it. When we came back, we were laughing and telling Andy about how much fun it was and how we wished he had been able to go. Soon after that, he quit one of the soccer teams, so he could go with us. I'm glad he did. Andy can bring fun to any activity.

Sunday was known as family day in our house through elementary school, though *family day* wasn't always a popular term. Sundays were protected. They couldn't have friends over or go to another friend's home unless it was a birthday party. Ed and I knew how little time we had to make the bonds of our family strong; to do that required spending time together.

We bought an aboveground pool. There is nothing like a cannonball next to your brothers to bring you close together. We tried badminton, and Ben sprained his ankle. We had an older RV, and on Sunday afternoons, we would load the kids and the dogs and drive to the Dairy Queen in the next town. We would get our meal and eat in the RV. Even the dogs were treated to an ice cream or a burger.

Then there were the Sundays we stayed home and did nothing!

"We aren't doing anything. Why can't Brandon come over?" Andy would shuffle the soccer ball between his feet, wearing his best pitiful look. "He can practice with me."

"So ask one of your brothers to play," Ed would say.

"Never mind." Andy would take the ball to his room. "They don't play soccer."

Ben didn't seem to mind staying home. He would rather play video games.

When Josh started asking for friends to come and play on Sundays, both older boys had no trouble shouting, "It's family day! No one is allowed to come over."

By the time Ben and Andy were in their teens, we revised the rule. We realized having their friends come to our house gave us the opportunity to know who they were hanging out with the rest of the week. That turned out to be one of our success stories. As the boys grew older, they began working at the business. We hired some of their friends. Ed was able to interact with his sons and their friends in a unique way. Some of those boys—now men—stop by our house to say hi, give me a hug, and check the fridge when they come into town.

"You have received the Spirit of adoption as sons, by whom we cry, 'Abba! Father!' " (Romans 8:15)

All of us take comfort in the familiar. Even individuals who pride themselves on being untraditional have some things in their lives that border on ritual. Maybe it's what they eat for Friday supper, the spot where the blanket is spread for each Memorial Day picnic, or the side of the church to which they gravitate Sunday after Sunday. Heaven forbid a visitor be uninformed regarding assigned seating in that favored pew! Or worse yet, a new member claims that spot as their own, and the hunt for a new seat is on, maybe even a migration to the other side of the sanctuary. Changes in routine can be very disconcerting.

Changes, like moving and remarrying, give the opportunity to review those traditions to which we cling. Ritual and routine can be a comfort and bring unity to a family. Sometimes. At other times, we become slaves to our routines and traditions, even though they may no longer serve us as they did when first begun. Parents can choose which traditions to keep and which to set aside, embracing new beginnings in many areas of life.

Diana and Ed adopted each other's family rituals, as they had adopted their boys. But the boys were keepers. Some of the family rituals required editing as time passed and the boys grew and gathered friends like dust bunnies.

LOSE THE LUTEFISK

Do you feel bound to observe traditions that bring nothing but grief? The American family in which I grew up was a proud member of the Sons of Norway and Daughters of Valhalla. I am a third-generation Norwegian American—all Norwegian! We celebrated Christ's birth on Christmas Eve, danced around the Christmas tree, sang "Ja Er Sa Glad," and my mother served lutefisk, a traditionally preserved and prepared cod fish dish. Sometimes, at my father's urging, she would serve lutefisk at Thanksgiving and Easter too. Finding the lutefisk was always quite an ordeal, as not many proprietors even know what it is.

To make the cod edible (which is a relative term), it is soaked for four to six days in cold water. When the soak is complete, your lutefisk is ready to steam and serve, smelling up the house for days.

My husband, also of Norwegian ancestry, had never eaten lutefisk until we began dating. His dad was a Son of Norway, but his mom had Hungarian roots and wasn't interested in preparing lutefisk. I'll never forget the look on my husband's face when he joined my family for Christmas Eve that first time and bravely stabbed a forkful of lutefisk. His eyes got big as he chewed, chewed, and chewed some more. Needless to say, once we married, my husband and I banded together in an anti-lutefisk alliance, our goal to lose the lutefisk and serve it no more. Every year, my dad would ask, "Did you find the lutefisk?" I never did.

Do the traditions you cherish bond your family or cause discord? Common family traditions to reevaluate include:

Rituals Surrounding Gift Giving: If exchanging gifts with your growing nuclear and extended family is beyond your means, perhaps it's time to introduce the practice of drawing one name rather than buying for all family members. This is good stewardship. In most cases, even family members who initially complain about the change in the number of gifts given and received will one day say, "Thank you."

Birthday Celebrations: If you have been over-the-top in the gift-giving department, maybe it's time to think about a more conservative approach. Seize the opportunity to pull birthday celebrations into perspective and make them manageable. Most families have financial concerns and limited monetary resources. Modeling and practicing good stewardship is an important lesson for our children.

Weekends: The weekend plans of families blended due to divorce may take on a competitive edge. When this happens, we lose sight of the purpose for our gatherings, and we often forfeit the joy those meetings once brought. Our gatherings may become tedious. Small changes in weekend routines may be the place to start introducing schedule changes to your family. Consider starting with the elimination of one item on the family calendar. Bracket the item on your calendar, and discuss with your family what, if anything, will be selected in its place. Perhaps family reading or game playing will appear in its place. Perhaps that bracketed hour will become personal health time. Consider spending that hour in service to God and the community. Selecting a family servant project to support is an excellent way for families to grow and mature in faith and in service to their Lord.

While they may not be traditions, some of our familiar routines may warrant rewriting as time passes. Ed and Diana made a deliberate choice to attend their boys' activities. The boys were limited, each having a modest number of extra activities. Multiply that modest number times three, and the number of extra activities increases exponentially. A wall calendar with squares large enough that family members can list the activities in which they will participate is an easy, inexpensive organizational tool.

When keeping pace with a houseful of boys playing soccer, fencing, going to Scouts, taking gymnastics, piano, drums, or swimming, you'll find those family weekends quickly disappear or turn into something ugly! Staying appropriately connected to preteen and teenage children during the years when they are growing in independence is challenging. Diana and Ed loosened some of their restrictions regarding exclusive family Sundays. This created an open door—and refrigerator—to many of Andy, Ben, and Josh's friends. It also gave Ed and Diana the opportunity to be more vigilant parents while getting to know their children's friends.

Offering a gathering place to your children's friends may mean you spend more on groceries, you seldom have a home as neat as you would like, and you may have long periods of sleep deprivation. Research has recently proven what parents have known for decades: teenagers' sleep patterns are different than those of their parents. This comes as no surprise to those of us who have endured the repetitive thump of the bass booster, the smell of pepperoni, and raucous laughter or giggling late into the night. You may be tired, but you know where they are, and you know they are safe.

Those of you who welcome your sons' and daughters' teenage friends also have the honor of walking alongside these young people as they grow and mature. And it is a privilege. Yours may be the number your son's buddy calls when he learns his mom is sick, or his dad's been laid off, or his sister has graduated magna cum laude. Yours may be the fridge raided when they are in town for a brief visit. You may be the one who gets the hug. That would be a nice tradition.

> *"Oh sing to the LORD a new song, for He has done marvelous things!" (Psalm 98:1)*

17

Negotiating Who Gets Face Time in the Family Gallery

Family photos can cause an explosion of emotion. The wedding photos, baby photos, McDonald's birthday parties photos—the list goes on. Even the everyday snapshots of summer can bring you to your knees while you reach for a box of tissues. Those fractions of time move from beyond that moment to the ones before and after. Could I have done something different? Was it as fun as I remember it? What do the kids remember about this?

Both of our homes had walls dedicated to family pictures. Department and discount store photographers had our kids sitting in washtubs, holding balls, or posing in front of a colorful fall tree backdrop. My wall had family shots with John along with my mom and brother. My photos had to come down since I was moving. I packed them away, not quite sure if I should remove them from the frames or not. I decided to leave them framed.

Ed's photo timeline was more difficult to remove. What would Andy think when we took the photos down? Would he feel displaced when we moved in because the wall space where his smiling face had dominated would now be shared with two others?

Ed hadn't even asked me to marry him yet, but I knew he was planning to ask me in January. On New Year's Eve, he was hosting an "end of the decade" party for his friends. He used that excuse to take down the photos. The walls needed to be empty for him to hang long, blank sheets of paper for his guests to write down things that they remembered occurring in the last decade. After the party, he didn't hang the photos back on the wall. Instead, he put them in a box in the closet. Andy didn't seem to notice.

We knew we wanted the boys to remember Old Mom and Old Dad in their better days, unaffected by the changes that came from the cancer. We made sure each child had a 4 x 6 inch framed photo to put on their dressers in their bedroom. If they had asked for more photos, we would have made them available to them. They didn't ask. Time filled up those spaces with trophies, books, and toys, leaving no space for even a family photo of our new family.

We had boxes of photos and photo albums filled with our past lives. We kept them in a trunk in the living room. The lid of the trunk was kid friendly, which made it easy for any of the boys to access the treasure trove of memories at any time they wished. That happened about three times. They didn't seem to be interested in the past, only in what was for dinner and if they could go somewhere.

Once, Ed and I discussed lining the stairwell with pictures from before our marriage to the present. We couldn't decide what to do. Would that confuse the boys? Would it make them think of their old parents as perfect?

Then I cleaned out the top shelf of the kitchen cabinet and found photos of Debbi. Ed and Debbi had had a friend who wanted to open his own portrait studio, so he asked her to model for him.

The photos were beautiful, but she was wearing a two-piece bathing suit, and she had the physique of a twenty-year-old. I no longer did. There weren't bags under her eyes, and she was tanned—no sock lines from hanging out on the soccer fields. Her face held no wrinkles. She would forever be this stunning.

I asked Ed to do something with those photos. I didn't know what he did with them. I didn't really care, as long as they never graced the walls of our home. I couldn't compete with someone who never aged or gained a pound. Consequently, that is the same Debbi that has often appeared in my dreams, asking me to leave, so she could have her husband and child back. It had all been a mistake; she hadn't really died.

I realize that while Debbi looked good on paper, she wasn't here to experience Andy's life, and I was. Knowing how much she loved him and dreaded not recovering from the cancer was heartbreaking, but I knew if we put photos of Debbi and John on the wall, it would only bring discord between Ed and me. Neither of us could live up to the standards of the perfect person on glossy 8 x 10s. We needed to have our current life reflected back to us, so we could dream of our future.

It is still difficult to look back through those photos from before I married Ed. I can see the changes in John's facial expressions, usually anger or confusion. Then there are those where he is riding our horse with Ben, and that makes me smile, and I want Ben to see it. Or the one of Josh in his Old Dad's boots standing next to John.

The photos of Debbi holding Andy as an infant, or helping him blow out the candles on his cake, are equally challenging for me. I'm glad she was able to share those moments with him, yet I feel left out knowing I missed seven years of his life.

Ed has regrets of not taking photos of Debbi in the hospital to show Andy that she was in the hospital. Debbi requested that he not take any. She didn't want Andy to see her with tubes in her arms. Ed feels that if he had not acquiesced to her feelings, it might have been easier for Andy to understand what happened to his mom. She looked healthy when she left, and then she didn't return.

When we first got married, we tried to continue to bring John and Debbi into conversations with the boys. We would say, "Andy, do you remember how much your Old Mom loved olives?" or "Ben and Josh, do you remember when your Old Dad held you in front of him while you rode Scout, our horse, together?" After awhile, though, real life took over, and Debbi and John remembrances faded behind our new life. Ed and I decided we needed to do something about that.

When each of the boys turned twelve, we sat them down individually for a discussion. Ben was first to hit the magic age. I told him about his dad, about the good times and some of the not-so-good times when John was ill. I didn't know how much Ben remembered about those times. It seemed a good idea to explain things he had previously been too young to understand. Most of all, I wanted to stress both his heritage and the love John had for him. Ben listened carefully to what was said. He had a few questions like, "Did Old Dad have a temper like me?" and "Do you think I'll be as tall as he was?" The answer to both of those questions was "Yes." When he seemed to be finished asking, I told him he could always ask me questions, and I would be happy to tell him anything that wasn't private between his Old Dad and me.

Andy reacted differently to Ed. If it is possible to close yourself off to hearing the dialogue of another person without putting your fingers in your ears, that's what he did. He wouldn't look at

Ed. It was frustrating for Ed because he wanted Andy to hear the words, "Your mom loved you." He wanted to stress once again that it wasn't her choice to leave him.

Andy just wanted to know if Ed was done telling him things he didn't want to know. That didn't get him off the couch any faster. Ed continued to talk to him until he could tell Andy was listening. How? He made him repeat what he said. He was also encouraged to ask questions at any time. Recently he has started to ask about his Old Mom.

I'm not sure what is best in this situation. Ed and I both feel we handled the photos incorrectly. When we walk into homes of others, we are often stunned by the visual heritage represented on walls. We didn't put up photos of cousins and grandparents because there were so many. Our focus was so strongly centered on our nuclear family, wanting it to be perfect, and yet we didn't do family portraits. Were we afraid that if we did, our family would dissolve like the last ones? We aren't sure what our reason was, but it is a regret that we didn't have more of them taken.

And those photos that came off the wall in their frames? Those are still in the box.

"I thank my God in all my remembrance of you."
(Philippians 1:3)

Pictures in boxes, photos in closets, memories stored in chests and tucked away. Diana worked so hard to keep the painful memories at bay. To these efforts, she wanted the images prominently displayed in her home to reflect her family, the family she and Ed had built together—her blended family. Ed and Diana affirmed the importance of the "Old Mom" and the "Old Dad" in the lives of their sons. But each spouse was deeply wounded by the suffering from John and Debbi's terminal illnesses. So the pictures were in storage, but not the pain. The pain surfaced in ways that we see woven throughout the pages of this book.

What do you do with all the pictures accumulated during a marriage? How do you store those memories? I suspect that the conflict Diana experienced as she considered which pictures to hang in the family gallery may have been more easily resolved had there been no bereaved children to consider. The boys had photos of their deceased parents in their rooms, but the pictures in the family's shared living space was reserved for images of Josh, Ben, Andy, Diana, and Ed. The painful photographic reminders of love and loss were put away.

Many families do as Diana and shove the pictures that capture impressions from the past into dark corners. Often, the memories are dealt with similarly, pushed into corners of our minds. Licensed counselor and bereavement specialist Greg DeNeal recounts his own experience in the family gallery of his childhood home. During a typical childhood tussle, Greg careened off the hallway picture gallery. His smiling baby picture fell to the floor, frame splitting open, contents spilling out. As Greg bent to clean up the mess, he realized there was an additional photo that had been housed in the frame behind his. A picture of a kid that Greg didn't know had been stored in the same frame.

Greg brought the frame and its contents, along with the mystery, to his mother. He learned from his mother that the other photo in the frame was of Greg's older brother. The boy had died before Greg was born. Sadly, his big brother had died of a sudden illness. Greg's mother and father responded to their deep grief by erasing from their home all evidence of the son who had died. There were no pictures displaying his image, and the fact of his existence was a painfully kept secret.

He had many questions about the secret photo stored behind his own and the brother he had never known. His parents' response to the death of his older brother puzzled him. In later years, Greg would experience heartache himself, including the deaths of his father, mother, and beloved teenage son, Jeremy.

Talking about loss helped. Remembering helped. Greg's experience of mourning and his path toward healing have led him into ministry to the bereaved through individual and family counseling, facilitation of group seminars, and conferences.

In the conferences he leads, Greg informs participants that each of our losses has a story too. Our stories of loss have purpose and meaning, and there are reasons we carry our memories. Telling the story helps us to heal. Sometimes we try to keep sorrow at bay by putting away our memories and the proof of those memories, like pictures and mementos. Greg discovered that he didn't have to put the pictures or the memories of deceased loved ones away. He could tell their stories and share the important role those loved ones played in his life, remembering what each had meant to him. He didn't have to put them away.[1]

What happens when you have done as Diana and Ed and put the memories away? Years ago, when I was working in a seminary counseling center, the wife of a seminarian and mother of three came to see me. Sallie (not her real name) was struggling with depression, or so she thought. "I shouldn't feel sad," she cried. "My husband had a wonderful internship year. He'll graduate in a few months. My life is good." The tears streamed down her face.

Sallie's family history revealed she was approaching the tenth anniversary of her father's death. She had been in her ninth month of pregnancy and living hundreds of miles from him when her dad died. Sallie's doctor prohibited travel, so she was unable to be with her father in his last days or attend his funeral. She grieved that she wasn't at his bedside and that her children never knew their grandfather.

I asked Sallie what her father would have thought of the direction she and her husband were heading: into parish ministry. Sallie was sure her father would have been very proud.

In the coming weeks, I asked Sallie to bring a picture of her father. She brought in a couple of pictures she had dug out from a box stored under her bed. On the day she arrived for counseling, she was smiling and appeared much more relaxed.

She described what had happened as she sorted through the box she had pulled out from under the bed. Her kids gathered round, and Sallie sorted through the photos. "This is your grandpa…his favorite car…here we are on a family vacation." She laughed; the children giggled. They got to know their grandpa as they looked together at their mom's treasured photos.

Most couples do not prominently display pictures of previous spouses. Children, however, need permission to treasure both parents and display pictures of all family members in their rooms. If your blended family has experienced divorce, this may mean you take the high road for the benefit of your son or daughter, dusting around your child's family gallery, which may include pictures of stepsiblings, your ex, and of course, those who live in your home.

You may have to swallow hard when listening to your child recount the activities he or she enjoys when with the other parent. Should you become concerned regarding the appropriateness of events your child has experienced, run your concerns past a trustworthy, objective individual like your pastor.

Many people try to distance themselves from painful events. Frequently, we push the reminders of our pain away, just as we stash photos in closets or shove our memories under beds. We don't speak of our losses and in so doing, establish a pattern of avoidance that indicates our children should remain silent also.

This robs our families of the privilege of acknowledging how they have loved and been loved by other significant people, and we risk sending the message that they should not grieve, should not love, and should not hurt.

But Christ, our Savior, wept at the pain of loss. And it is His strength that enables families to face grief and separation, His strength that facilitates healing, even blending a new family unit from two broken ones. New family galleries develop in the homes of blended families. We may not hang every picture in the same way it was hung in our earlier family homes, but we don't have to keep those pictures in the closet either.

"Comfort, comfort My people, says your God."
(Isaiah 40:1)

18

Vacations,
or Don't Touch Mine!

Our first year of marriage had flown by, and the end of the school year was approaching. It was time to think of getting away for awhile. But where?

I had been going to Table Rock Lake in Missouri since I was seventeen. I liked the idea of going back to the same place every year, building memories around a place. It was comfortable knowing what to expect, what the water temperature would be, and what activities were available. I wanted to continue that; maybe not the same cabins, but there would be other places we could rent.

"No," Ed shook his head. "We should do something different. There's a lot of this country to explore, and I want the boys to experience all of it."

"No lake?" Hysteria bubbled in my stomach. I didn't know how to pack and plan for a vacation away from the lake. Hadn't that been obvious on our honeymoon? It was snowing in the mountains in June, and we didn't bring gloves!

"Come on," Ed grabbed my hands. "Be adventurous. It will be fun; you'll see."

What I saw was hours of driving and kids fighting in the backseat. "I think we should go to the lake. It's only a six-hour drive from here. It could be our place, and when the boys get married, they can come and bring their kids. It'll be wonderful, just like a movie."

"One with the word *nightmare* in the title? Look at those boys. They like action and adventure. There's so much out there for them to see."

I used the one wife word that says it all. "Fine."

Our adventures took us from the East Coast to the West Coast. The first year, we went to Coco Beach and Disneyworld. It was fun, but I still longed to go to the lake. Several years later, we went to Michigan, and it felt like my memory of the lake. We stayed in a condo, played in the water, and toured the small towns close by. We took the boys water-skiing, and we did a puzzle together. I made some of our meals. It was even better than my remembered lake trip because it wasn't as hot. There was a screened-in porch where I could escape with a book, and at night, Ed and I could sit outside and watch the boats.

When it came time to plan the next year's vacation, I begged to go back to the same place. That year, time and money were short, and I was able to convince Ed to repeat a trip.

"We're going back to Michigan, boys!" I blurted out the hot news of the day at the dinner table.

"Where at?" Ben asked.

"Homestead, the place we went last year. Remember how much fun we had? Andy, you rode your skateboard down the big hill? Ben, you and Josh went to the pool every day?"

They all looked at Ed.

"Why are we doing the same thing, Dad?" Andy asked.

Ed arched an eyebrow. "Sometimes, boys, we need to do something your mom likes."

The trip was not fun. The boys didn't enjoy it. Josh said he never wanted to go back to that place again. I was crushed. Ed's adventurous personality had infected all of them.

On one of our date nights, we were at an RV show. We had been to several shows and thought owning an RV would be much easier than camping since we could leave it packed and leave when Ed had a free weekend. It would also be a cheaper way to travel with five people.

"Let's buy one." Ed sat behind the wheel of a $175,000 bus with a dreamy look on his face. I knew he wasn't thinking about me, more like the open road and sleeping passengers.

"Are you crazy? We don't have this kind of money."

"Not a new one. I bet we can find a used one we could afford."

"I don't know if this is such a good idea. Can't we just rent one and try it out? Besides, wouldn't this be like going to the same place every year? I wouldn't want to break your rule about that again."

"Think about it, a different place every night, no expensive hotel costs for five people, and we could take our own food. You and the boys could sleep in the morning while I drive, so there would be fewer arguments between the boys. We would save tons of money."

What I heard him say was no maid service, wet towels to dry somewhere, and I had to cook in a kitchen the size of a thimble. "I'm not sure. Wouldn't it just sit most of the year?"

"We would still save money. Besides, I want to do Laborers for Christ when the kids get older."

"What?" This was a new one, and anything involving labor I wasn't all that fond of, especially once the kids were gone. I was planning a future with a clean house, little laundry, and eating dinner out five nights a week.

"I've been thinking about it since they came and helped us build our church. You would like it. You like to paint; that can be your contribution." How I wished he didn't have brown eyes that hypnotized.

We bought a small RV. The first trip we took was to Montana. Once we were packed and on our way, everyone enjoyed the trip. Ed did make it easier for me by reserving a room at one of the lodges for a few days. The place we stayed didn't have a television; instead there were checkerboards and Ping-Pong tables.

That evening, the boys lined up at the window, looking out across the street where the RV was parked.

"Can't we go and sleep in the RV tonight?" Ben asked.

"Come on, Dad, just let us go. Mom can stay here. She just wants to read anyway."

Ed made them suffer through the next twenty-four hours without electronics, making the next day's drive pleasant, as they enjoyed the movies and video games again.

Then we took the Oregon Trail trip and, as Gary Smalley would say, those bad times build good memories. We had several, like breaking down on the highway and getting stranded in Kearney, Nebraska. We stayed in a hotel for two glorious days. There were no dishes to wash, no wet towels to dry, and I didn't have to cook once.

However, that unscheduled stop caused a kink in the plans. We had to drive almost nonstop to reach the coast. The boys were no longer content. They needed exercise and space away from each other. We stopped in a few places, like Chimney

Rock, so they could climb. There were a few other short stops, and it seemed that at all of them, there were informational signs about those who had taken the trail so many years ago. Many of them told stories of children left behind because they had wandered from the campsite, and there wasn't time to look for them. Sometimes those signs made me cry in sadness for those moms and dads. However, I will admit there were times I considered it might be nice to drive off and leave my three hellions, but only for a millisecond.

When Ben and Andy turned sixteen and had girlfriends, they didn't want to go on vacation, but they very generously offered to take care of our home and the pets if we wanted to go.

We didn't fall for that. We stayed home and did day trips, inviting their girlfriends along on all of the activities. We gave each son some money to spend, either to buy souvenirs or to use during the week on dates. It turned out to be more fun than most of us thought it would be. There were areas of St. Louis neither the boys nor I had been to before. Even Ed was treated to the new City Museum that had just opened its doors. We ate at Blueberry Hill, and the kids played checkers while waiting for their burgers. In the hot afternoon, we would come home and swim in our pool. We also had a satellite dish installed, so Josh could watch the Disney channel. We tried to make it feel like a real vacation—with the bonus of not having to pack clothes and sleeping in our own beds.

That experience worked so well that we continued to take their friends with us on vacations. Girlfriends got their own rooms!

"Restore us, O Lord God of Hosts! Let Your face shine."
(Psalm 80:19)

My husband and I can recount vacations with our parents, memories that bring us laughter and tears, maybe even a memory of frustration and family strife. My mom and dad may have wanted to drive off without me when it was time to head home a time or two, but somehow, we always returned home together.

Diana and Ed were practicing the art of negotiation with the planning of each vacation. They were indeed building family memories. In some cases, the trial and error involved in trying new experiences resulted in memories that had the family laughing long after they returned home.

Ed and Diana desired to strengthen the family through their shared travels. They faced the challenges blended and non-blended families experience traveling in close quarters for an extended period of time. (I recall that when car shopping, I stipulated that our minivan required captain's seats throughout, so our children couldn't touch one another. It didn't work. They found ways to poke one another.) The couple is to be applauded for seeking out economical ways for their family to have vacations. Blended families affected by shared custody requirements may not be able to load up the motor home and spend two or three weeks on the road, but they can manage meaningful and fun vacations. Some other tips for blended family vacations include:

Keep It Short

If you are a newly blended family and planning your first vacation together, consider a short trip. Even in traditional families, members wear on one another after a period of time, particularly if vacationing in close quarters. Choosing destinations that don't require too much travel time and staying for two or three days may be less stressful for those traveling for the first time together than planning a month-long family camping trip—in tents—in the first month of your marriage.

Consider a Stay-cation

Some families find enjoyment staying at home and planning day trips. This is another good option for the newly blended family. Parents take vacation time but, rather than incur the expense of hotels, choose a destination within a day's drive of home.

You might spend the day at the zoo, museums, historical sites, a nearby lake, or water park and return home at night. Family members can decompress in familiar surroundings and sleep in their own beds! When planning a stay-cation, parents can present a variety of pre-approved options to the children, and each child may select his or her favorite "trip." Because they are economical and can be adapted to less flexible work and vacation schedules, some established blended families will choose stay-cations even after enjoying successful traditional vacations.

Keep It Simple

Newly blended family members need time to get used to one another. If this is your first trip together, a short vacation may be more successful than a long trip. Save longer trips for later, after your kids have been together over a year. Also, consider saving complicated itineraries for later, after the family has had some time to grow together and knows a little more what to expect from one another day-to-day.

Don't Over-schedule

A less complicated itinerary allows the family to stretch together and accommodate challenges that come up. Allowing wiggle room in your schedule permits you to spend extra time at the beach if your family is having a great time and getting along well. Also, there is a greater chance that you will remain calm during minor crises, like hunting for that missing sandal or lost map.

Have Realistic Expectations

Vacations can be joyful, restful, educational, all kinds of things. But no vacation will be perfect. Be realistic about your vacation and the sinful human beings who will be participating—parents and children. Two-year-olds will still melt down when they miss naps, children who reside in another home will miss the parent and siblings who are not present, moms and dads will be crabby when they are sleep deprived, and family members will be disappointed if it rains every day you plan to go to the beach. If you expect a perfect outcome, you will be disappointed.

Be Flexible

Our plans rarely go exactly as we intend, on vacation or just about any other activity. Vacations are supposed to be fun and refreshing—for all family members. Rigid scheduling and an inability to go with the flow can take the fun out of a family getaway. Good, realistic planning at the front end may enable you to be more flexible as your vacation progresses.

Leave Room for Downtime

It is not unusual for parents who have scheduled vacations too tightly to return home feeling frazzled. Then when they return to work, rather than feeling refreshed, they make comments like, "I need a vacation to recover from my vacation!" Planning a "blank" day or two post-vacation can help minimize the chance that you or your spouse will make such a statement. That day home following your vacation allows for decompression and gives kids and parents the opportunity to leisurely return to normal activities. Children might check in with friends or enjoy some quiet time, and parents may take a slower approach to resuming daily chores, such as laundry and yard work.

Accommodations for Children with Multiple Sets of Parents

- Give specific information regarding travel plans to the other biological parent.

- Respect all legal custody arrangements.

- Try to honor a uniform schedule between households.

- Maintain consistency regarding your household rules, even if the number of residents changes as children come and go. Rules should remain constant, even when you are on vacation, at home or away.

- Perhaps your "vacation" means that a child whose primary residence is with the other parent comes to spend time in your home. You might plan an exciting trip. But if you don't have much time together during the rest of the year, a stay-cation may enable you to have more quiet time with your visiting child or children.

Wrap your travel plans, vacation itineraries, and stay-cations in prayer.

Vaya con Dios–go with God!

> *"And the Lord will guide you continually."* (Isaiah 58:11)

19

Is It Possible God Wants Me Here?

So many times during that first year of marriage, I wanted to run, pack up Ben and Josh, and flee back to Missouri. I still had my house. I didn't even care if I had my belongings. Just my kids and me—that was all I needed. I didn't like all the drama and anxiety that percolated through my veins.

I had used all my mothering skills and teaching abilities on Andy. I was broken, and Ed and I hadn't made it to our first anniversary yet.

"Mom, aren't you going to go get him?" Ben paced in front of me.

"He hasn't gone far. I can see him under the pine trees. He'll get hungry soon and come home." I gave him a hug. "He's come back every time so far, hasn't he? And I'm watching to make sure he doesn't go any farther. Go play with Josh."

Ben took Josh into his room to play. I stood watch at the back door, my stomach twisted and squeezed. This was the third time this week Andy had run away from home. He didn't like or understand the need to live by my rules of order. They weren't hard rules, nothing out of the ordinary. This particular day, I had asked him to put his cereal bowl in the dishwasher. His response was to tell me that was my job; that's why his dad married me. Wives are supposed to do all the work, not the kids.

Soon there was movement under the grove of pine trees. I tensed. Would he go farther this time? Would I have to chase him down and hold him tight, so he couldn't run? My shoulders sagged. The weight lifted for the moment as he turned and made his way into the house.

There was a power struggle between us for Ed's affection. I knew Andy felt displaced by me, but I didn't know how to change his feelings. We tried several counselors; one suggested I spend an hour a day with Andy only—doing things he enjoyed. Go for a walk or bike ride, maybe take him to lunch. Lovely thought, but I had two other children. If I spent an hour with Andy, then I needed to spend an hour with each of the other two. That made three hours out of my day—every day. The psychologist didn't have a suggestion of what I could do with the two who weren't spending time with me. We didn't go back to see that psychologist.

I did try to squeeze in alone times. I surprised him at school and took him out for lunch, and then he asked me not to do that anymore because he couldn't play with his friends. I asked Ed to watch the other two and took Andy to do errands. Again he asked me not take him anymore; he would rather be home. The one thing we did do together that worked was making cookies.

Andy continued to resist my rules, along with Ed's. The difference between Ed and me was Grand Canyon-size. I would become defensive and more authoritarian as Andy dragged me from the present discussion to other arguments and grievances from the past. Ed would keep Andy centered on the current situation, always bringing Andy back to the problem in front of him until Andy would give up the argument or be sent to his room. It was exhausting.

As he grew older, the intensity grew. I tried giving him a notebook, thinking we could start a conversation on paper by slipping the notebook back and forth. He wrote, "I don't have anything to write, and I don't want to do this."

After one horrible argument, I ended up in Andy's room. I told him no matter how hard he tried, he didn't have the power to make me leave. I was staying, and he might as well adapt. I was his mom now, and I loved him. Andy didn't have anything to say, so I left the room. While he was at school, I would go sit on his bed and pray for him, for us, and for our relationship to change.

By the time he was fifteen, our relationship consisted of "stay out of my way, I'll stay out of yours, and everything will be fine." Except it wasn't.

One incident in particular is hard to write about. I have forgiven Andy and wanted to forget about it, but I think it might help someone in a similar situation. So after getting Andy's permission, I am free to tell what happened.

We were arguing in the car. I needed him to watch Josh that night, but he had made his own plans without asking us. We were less than a hundred yards from the garage. If we could just get there, I could get away from him. I don't remember what Andy said, but I know that it topped my frustration meter, and I reached over and smacked him in the chest, yelling, "Stop it!"

Andy retaliated by hitting me with his fist. I slammed the car to a stop, still not at the driveway, and made him get out of the car.

Ed happened to pull into the driveway behind me. When I told him what had happened, he was angry but wasn't sure how to handle the situation. He didn't say much, grounded Andy, and made him watch Josh while we went out that night with our pastor and his wife.

Ed ate his dinner and conversed with them as if nothing was wrong. I did my best to keep a smile on my face, hoping I was able to hide my worry about taking care of Josh that evening. I was afraid Andy would hurt him. I didn't want anyone to know what a horrible mom I was to my son.

We made an appointment to see a counselor but only went once. We should have kept going because the next few years were difficult. Andy continued doing poorly in school, refusing to take his ADD medication. In college, he would take a class, drop it, and have to pay us back.

Many times I wanted to leave. I was afraid of Andy's temper and never comfortable living with him after that. What stopped me was my promise to the judge—Andy is my son. My wedding ring has three stones, one for each child, reminding me of the vow I made to God: to love and cherish my husband and my family no matter what. God wanted me in this family. He knew Andy needed a mom who would stick out the hard times, even if she wanted to run.

Today, Andy and I have a terrific relationship. He's found his place in the world. Art is his passion, and he has two master's degrees from Fontbonne University. He calls to check on me when his dad is out of town. He always gives me a hug when he sees me and when he leaves. He does say he'll never have children because he doesn't want to be treated the way he treated us. I hope he changes his mind because Andy is an awesome son. I loved him then, and I love him now.

"Remembering before our God and Father your work of faith and labor of love and steadfastness of hope in our Lord Jesus Christ." (1 Thessalonians 1:3)

For the third time in a week, Andy had run away. He didn't go far, and he always returned. His behavior certainly tried Diana's patience and tested her on many levels. Maybe that was the point. Did Andy truly want to run, or did he wonder if Diana would *really* come after him? How far would she let him go? Would he lose another mother? Would Diana pass the test? Or was Andy concerned that in accepting Diana, he was rejecting the importance his deceased mom had held in his life? We don't know the answer to those questions; perhaps we never will. We do know that there was a struggle afoot.

Power struggles are no surprise to a blended family home. Diana remembers how hard that first year of marriage was. Most blended families report the first year is the most difficult period. With that in mind, it is realistic to expect that children, especially adolescents, will exhibit some sort of rebellion and some degree of anger. Recognizing that rebellion and/or anger will likely be manifested at some point is a heads-up to parents and step-parents. Much has been written about rebellion and teenage angst disrupting intact families. Andy was only nine! His behavior, exasperating as it was for Diana, was not unusual for a child adjusting to a new family coming to live in his home, sharing his space, bringing new rules and new routines. So, while some contrary behavior is typically demonstrated by rebellious and angry kids and teens in non-blended families, rebellion among kids who are transitioning through the family blending process often increases dramatically.

Andy challenged Diana. She questioned God and wondered if this life, this town, this family, was truly God's plan for her and her boys. Moments of uncertainty are normal and experienced by many parents facing stressful adjustment periods. Moments of uncertainty can become deeply painful and are frequently accompanied by a burden of guilt and insecurity. Those insecure, guilty thoughts and feelings do funny things to people.

Often we turn inward, guilt turns to shame, and we become immobilized by these burdens. There is a place for our guilt and shame, a place for all the burdens that weigh our spirits and break our hearts. That place is at the foot of the cross. Christ hears the cries of our hearts. The plea for forgiveness of our dark thoughts and harsh behaviors will be heard. You are not alone! Christ hears, Christ forgives, and Christ strengthens us to go on.

CONNECTIONS AND SUPPORT

Patience may wear thin during the beginning phases of your family's blending. Please hang on! If you become an "empty vessel," you cannot serve your family. Care well for yourselves. There are numerous support opportunities. Diana reports some less than satisfying visits to a counselor. Please be encouraged that counseling *can* be helpful. Be an informed consumer of counseling services: consider a marriage and family therapist who has experience working with blended families. If you are searching for a counselor, try one of the following methods:

- **Your insurance carrier**—Most insurance companies provide directories that include information regarding office locations, specialties, and level of experience.

- **Local clergy**—Your pastor may have a resource file and knowledge of area mental health counselors who have successfully walked alongside struggling congregants. Some pastors and counselors will work together to triage spiritual and clinical counseling. Pastors may also know which area churches offer support groups for adults and children.

- **Hospital networks**—Area hospitals often offer support groups for families. Support groups provide guidance, equip with resources, and help participants recognize that they are not alone.

- **Friends**—A personal recommendation from someone who has "walked the walk" is worth more than a profile printed on paper.

- **Professional registries**—Organizations like the American Association of Christian Counselors (www.aacc.net) enable you to search by zip code for services close to home. Directories may include biographical information and links to provider Web sites.

- **Bible study groups**—Perhaps participation in a Bible study for blended families would be of greater help than professional counseling. Contact your local ministerial alliance or district directory.

Be an informed consumer. Ask questions. Read between the lines when reviewing professional profiles listed on public registries. Perhaps you and your spouse are committed to finding a Christian clinician but want to choose a provider from among those listed on your insurance.

Be alert to profiles of therapists who describe themselves as Christian counselors and list GLBT (Gay/Lesbian/Bisexual/Transgendered) as a specialty, or the local abortion clinic as an alternate clinical site. They may be fine clinicians, but these practitioners may not define issues of faith in the same manner as you do. I write this because listings such as these are transparent, but clients who have not understood or discerned the content accurately often feel misled.

Again, you are a consumer. A critical piece to effective counseling is the relationship established between client and counselor. If a counselor isn't a good fit, find one who is. Professionals recognize that they will not be able to help every client who signs a "Consent to Treat" form. Discussing your questions and concerns with your therapist can be an important part of the therapeutic process.

Diana was frustrated by her counselor's recommendation that she spend one hour per day alone with Andy. Remember that you own your therapy hour, so speak up about recommendations that cannot work, given your family dynamics. As a therapist, I understand that this counselor may have wanted to underline her concern that Andy and Diana build connection outside the lines drawn by conflict. As a parent seeking to provide equitable care to all the boys, the time designation—one hour per day—became the focus of Diana's concern. The message Diana perceived was that the counselor did not at all understand the challenges she faced. Since these difficulties were what had led her to seek counseling, the counselor's lack of recognition caused Diana to despair that counseling could help her at all.

Diana's commitment to her blended family, though tested many times, held fast. She had made a promise before her God that she would be faithful to Ed and to their boys, Andy, Ben, and Josh. God *had* equipped her. She waited at the door for Andy, reassuring the other boys that it would be okay. She hoped. The hope Diana had for Andy, for Josh and Ben, and for the family formed by her marriage to Ed, was not based on her abilities as a wife and mother. Diana's hope rested in her God to guide, empower, and forgive.

> "And He who searches hearts knows what is the mind of the Spirit." (Romans 8:27)

20

Performance Anxiety for Parents and Kids

Did I mention that Andy and Ben are twenty-one days apart in age? I'm sure I have, but I wanted to restate it so you have a fresh picture of two bubbly eight-year-olds in your mind as we started our blending process. One boy with cute, spiky hair, and the other with a shaved head. Yes, I said shaved.

In the van, Andy had challenged Ben to get his head shaved. If Ben would do it, so would he. I suggested it might not be a good idea, as their heads would get sunburned at the pool. It didn't matter what I said; they both thought they would look great and wouldn't have to comb or wash their hair.

Ben went to the chair first and had all of his beautiful blond hair shaved. He was almost bald. His scalp was bright white next to his tanned face. Andy's eyes widened as they took in the expanse of scalp. He looked pensive as he trotted off to get his own head shaved.

Except he didn't. He came back with most of his hair.

"Why didn't you do it?" Ben ran his hand across his scalp.

"I didn't know heads were ugly. I didn't want to do that." Andy grinned.

My mother reaction was to yank Andy back in and shave his head myself. I restrained myself by focusing on Ben, trying to reassure him. "Ben, you'll love having less hair this summer. You'll be much cooler than Andy." I was counting the days until school started, relieved that there would be time for his hair to grow before his first day at his new school. And before picture day. The ease the two of them had with each other before we were a family had shifted to one of competition.

Ben and Andy weren't twins, but I felt as if they were. They didn't dress the same or act the same, but we had the same dilemmas parents of twins encounter—only I didn't have a support group.

They were both in the same Cub Scout den. This was great for us as parents: we dropped them off and picked them up at the same place and time every week. Then one evening, they brought home something evil. It was bad enough to make Ed shudder.

In his hands, Ed held the two packages of Pinewood Derby cars. Both boys were gazing at him with such hope and faith. They had a dad who would help them build their cars, cars that would win the race.

Ed felt sick inside because he knew no matter how well they built the cars, one of the boys' cars would run faster than the other. On Friday evening, they sat around the kitchen table with all the pieces. Ed explained the importance of aerodynamics, using enough graphite in the wheels, and making sure the cars weren't overweight. Ben absorbed every word. Andy wanted to know how soon he could paint his car red, and could he put designs on it?

Ed patiently worked with both boys, making suggestions about how much wood would need to be cut from the pinewood block. They went to their grandfather's house and used the band saw to cut the shapes, then came back home to sand the wood smooth. It was a long process—one that Ben seemed to enjoy. Andy wanted to speed ahead to the paint process. Ed showed them how to sand the tires, and they did a few trial runs to see how the cars would roll. Then it was time to paint. It took Ben about five minutes to paint his car blue. It took Andy over an hour to paint his red, complete with white designs. Both boys were confident their cars would be the fastest at the meet.

The day of the race arrived. Is it wrong for parents to pray their child's car doesn't win? Ed and I were both praying for failure, disqualification, even a fire drill. And most of all, we were praying they didn't have to put their cars in the same heat.

They both made it through the first heat and had to run their cars against each other. Ed and I held hands. I couldn't watch. I couldn't bear to see the disappointment on one of those faces. We made it through one heat, and both boys placed.

"I should feel great that the cars made it this far," Ed said. "Instead I'm praying the wheels come off. This is crazy."

They lined the cars on top the tracks. I squeezed Ed's hand tighter.

The cars sailed down the track. Andy's car beat Ben's.

It would only be worse now if Andy won. The next heat, we cheered for Andy; even Ben was cheering, but Andy's car didn't win. In this instance, the two boys were fine with the competition. We made it worse for ourselves.

BEN (AT AGE 27)

"Dad helped us build our cars. They were both similar in size and construction. I didn't even think about one being better than the other."

ANDY (AT AGE 27)

"Working with Dad was cool. He let us use tools and do the work ourselves. I was proud of my car and Ben's. I just hoped one of us would win."

In junior high, they were both in band: Andy played the trumpet and Ben the drums. The goal in band was to be first chair. Ben had been in band for several years and still hadn't advanced. Andy made first chair the first semester. Eventually, they both quit band. Andy went on to soccer in high school, and Ben stayed away from group activities.

When we registered Ben for elementary school, we asked that he and Andy not be put in the same homeroom class to allow them some autonomy. That meant they had separate friends. Andy had many because he is a social person. Ben had a select few friends. Once there was a discussion of "how many friends do you have" between them that became heated. I set them down and explained that each of them had different personalities, and it was okay to have a few friends or a lot of them.

Grades were a big issue. Ben always did well. He brought home papers to be signed for field trips, and he kept us informed of test dates. Andy didn't like school. He struggled with math and often forgot he was supposed to do his homework. By fifth grade, we had him tested for attention deficit disorder and put on Ritalin. Both his grades and his outlook on life improved, but he hated taking the medication because he said he couldn't feel anything. He asked me more than once if I would love him better if he took his medication. It was difficult for him to understand that I loved him even if he didn't take it, but his life was so much easier when he did. There were fewer arguments between us, he made the honor roll in eighth grade, and our family life was more peaceful. I didn't understand why he wouldn't want to take it.

I understand it now. Andy is an artist, not a communicator. The medication dulled his creativity. When he was taking art classes in high school, he quit taking his medication. His grades dropped to the point we weren't sure he would graduate. Which led to another problem: how do you have a graduation party for one son if the other didn't graduate? Ben said he didn't want a party, so we gave him money. Two days before graduation, Andy was told he would graduate but wouldn't get his diploma until he paid his library fine. Once he paid it, we gave him money too.

We wanted the boys to be more than family; we wanted them to be friends and to share friends and activities. It didn't happen while they were living at home. Now Andy takes his truck to Ben's house for help getting it fixed, and Andy's art graces Ben and his wife, Sara's, walls.

"Before I formed you in the womb I knew you."
(Jeremiah 1:5 NIV)

Ah, yes, the Pinewood Derby. I know that once the cars were race ready, Ed and Diana agonized that the boys might have difficulty with the realities of winning or losing. To understand the significance of the anxiety Ed might have experienced before the race, during construction of the cars, it helps to know where we live. Our respective families live in a lovely Norman Rockwell-type, small Midwest town located a few miles from a military Air Force base, and many residents of our community are active, on reserve, or retired from military service.

Scouting is serious business around here, and most of the local Scout leaders also fall into one of those previously noted military designations. My husband, Vern, is a civilian pastor. To Vern's relief, only one of our children participated in the Pinewood Derby—twice. The parents in our son's troop met with their Scouts at a dental office for several weeks prior to the event, where they helped their Cub Scouts use precision dental drills to craft their race cars. Eight-year-olds using precision dental drills!

Ed and Diana's fears about the competitive aspects of the Pinewood Derby were well founded. In my beloved community, parents frequently fueled an over-the-top attitude regarding this competition.

But not where Ed and Diana were concerned. They were troubled that elements of competition might disrupt the bond between their eight-year-old boys. These parents were vigilant to the differences in their children's temperaments, to their strengths, and their weaknesses.

Ed and Diana desired that their blended family not just share space, but bond. Andy, Ben, and Josh were related, brothers by adoption. It was their parents' prayer that the brothers be more than related, that they know and seek relationship with one another.

Fostering relationship is the deep longing of most parents guiding their children through the blending process. Parents long for relationship between siblings and stepsiblings and also between the children and themselves. How do we foster those sought-after relationships?

JAKE

"We have a loud, chaotic, wonderful house full of love and life. But it is very chaotic, and we really have to grab the little bits and pieces of one-on-one time we can. It can be a ride in the car when you find you only have one child, a trip to the grocery store, or something planned, like a movie or coffee break. It is a constant struggle to get alone time with each child. I don't know if there is ever enough, but we must try!"

Spend Time

Years later, when Diana asked Ben his recollections of the Pinewood Derby, he didn't even mention the outcome of the race. What was Ben and Andy's recollection of the Pinewood Derby? That their dad helped the boys build their cars. The fact that their dad was present and guided the boys in race car construction (and the use of power tools, no doubt) was the piece that left the imprint on Ben and Andy's minds. Showing up counts!

But not just for the big race. Relationships develop through many of the smallest parts of a family's day: sharing an after-school snack, meeting in the garage to tinker with tools, driving to band practice, getting a recap of a Sunday School lesson, helping select the right color paint for a project. Carve out a little time for each child on a regular basis. Show up.

PERFORMANCE ANXIETY FOR PARENTS AND KIDS

Recognize Your Child's Gifts

Diana knew her boys. She recognized the ways God had gifted Andy, Ben, and Josh individually. It is amazing to think that we are each crafted by God in unique fashion. Your children are different, and that is not an accident. We may have shared goals for our children and families—faith, health, and happiness—but we must recognize that their differences are to be celebrated. However, before we can assist our children in the nurture of their gifts, we need to recognize the unique aspects in our children's abilities and interests as gifts and blessings.

Nurture Unique Gifts

Andy is an artist. He has two master's degrees from a university with a prestigious art department. Ben is happily married, a homeowner, and works in the field of engineering. Josh is married and lives in Chicago, where he works as a businessman. Diana and Ed's sons know which brother to call when a car needs repairs, a blank space on a wall calls out for the right painting, or an electronic gadget is needed. The boys were always different. Their unique gifts were watered and tended.

Considering the ongoing nature vs. nurture discussion among child development specialists, it is fascinating to note that Andy, like Diana, his adoptive mother, is an artist. Ben and Josh, like Ed, their adoptive father, are in technical business fields. Interesting. Also interesting, on a personal level, is the fact that in the sixteen years that I have known them, this is the first time I have referred to Ed and Diana as adoptive parents to any of their boys.

They are a family.

Recognize Challenges

Sometimes what we see as struggles during childhood become strengths in adulthood. Daydreamers may have a hard time staying on task during class. Parents and teachers come alongside, identify the challenges, and provide assistance: a desk closer to the front of the class, a less distracting environment, encouragement that a child arrive at school well fed and equipped for the day, perhaps testing and assessment so that needs for medical intervention or tutoring may be determined and met.

That same daydreamer may grow to be a visionary software developer, a prominent painter, or an architect. Perhaps that dreamer will become a teacher gifted at recognizing the special needs of students, answering those needs, and teaching students in ways that recognize a child's challenge and match his or her style of learning.

Look for the Rainbow

Honest encouragement is vital to growing hearts and minds. Vital, also, is honest acknowledgement that we understand a child's disappointment and sorrow. Our children need to know we are strong enough to shoulder their grief. We model how we have grown through adversity. Our positive outlook helps children take hold of God-given resilience and the truth that there is a rainbow—hope through Christ.

A bald head *is* cooler in the summer and great for summer days at the swimming pool! And it's aerodynamic too. In an Air Force town, aerodynamics is really impressive. Just ask the winner of the Pinewood Derby!

> "We have this hope as an anchor for the soul, firm and secure." (Hebrews 6:19)

21

Picking Your Battles

Normal parents have to tell their children no when they ask to do something that will harm or disfigure them. So do parents of blended families. It just isn't as easy to do it. Sometimes you think, "If I let him do this, then I'll be the amazing parent, the one that said yes, the one that believed in him." You have to learn to say no and mean it when it counts. Ed often said to me as the children grew, "You need to pick your battles." He was right. There is almost always a bigger battle waiting around the corner to fight.

Andy was nine when he decided he absolutely had to have his ear pierced.

"No. You aren't doing that," I said.

"I have to. It's really cool."

Andy's animated face said it all. If I would allow just this one thing, I would be the best mom in the universe. It was tempting. Here was my chance to shine and to be the mom that Andy wanted. I could be the cool mom. *Just say yes. Go ahead. What could it hurt? After all, you have pierced ears.* I wanted to say yes. I wanted to be adored by this small boy, but I had to be responsible.

"No. It's not appropriate for a nine-year-old to have a pierced ear. None of your friends wear earrings."

"I know. I would be the first." Andy's bouncy energy could not be contained in his small body.

"The answer is still no."

"Then I'll do it myself." His eyes widened, and he jutted his chin a few inches higher. "I'll do it in the garage, with Dad's drill."

"Go upstairs to your room. End of discussion."

"But . . . " There is always a "but" with Andy. "Dad will let me."

"Upstairs, no piercings until you move out of the house."

"But that will be a long time."

"Yes, it will." I sighed, wishing I could speed up the clock.

Other influences trickled into our home via the Internet, and another battle ensued, this time with Ben. He had discovered pornography sites at the age of thirteen. He didn't think we would find out, but we did. I had set the settings on the Internet to track the time someone was online. The computer was off limits while Ed and I were on our weekly Friday date nights. The Internet account showed someone was spending most of that time online.

I checked the history and didn't recognize the sites listed. I clicked on one, then another and another. They were all adult sites; each of them asked me if I was 18. I was devastated. Even the first pages of these sites had photos of women no one should see. Which one of my older sons had been looking at these degrading images? In my heart I knew. So did Ed.

"It has to be Ben." Ed said.

"Are you sure?" I asked. "Why not Andy?"

Ed tilted his head. "Andy?"

"Yeah, I know, couldn't be him." He never went near the computer; video games, sure, but the computer he disliked. "So who's going to confront him?"

"I'll talk to him. I think it has to be me. He needs to know how to respect women, and he might be more comfortable asking me questions."

"Good, and make sure you take away every privilege he has forever."

"We'll take away the computer and the video games."

"So we won't be doing our date night? The babysitter must not be checking on them; we can't trust her to do that." I didn't want to give up that date night, but if it meant our son carried out his sentence, then I would.

"We have a secret weapon—Josh. He'll tell us if Ben uses the computer or plays Nintendo."

"Deal. But just in case, let's come home early this Friday, and don't tell him I know how to find out where he's been on the Internet."

Ben was curious about the opposite sex, and someone at school had told him how to search out the sites. He served his sentence, and we were wiser parents. Evil had invaded our house and been kicked to the curb, and we were on high alert to keep it from getting back in.

When Andy was sixteen, he found a creative outlet—the guitar. He joined a band, wrote music for them, and performed with several groups for a few years. He grew his hair long, and we didn't say anything. Then he wanted to get a tattoo.

The arguments were similar to the ear piercing ones we had had when he was younger, but much louder—and we couldn't send him to his room. We told him if he came home with one, it meant he had made an adult decision. The result would be that he would find himself living in an adult world. We wouldn't pay for college, and he would have to move out. Tattoos are permanent, and Andy's future was yet to be written. Depending on his choice of a career, having them prominently displayed could possibly keep him from obtaining a job he would like.

Then one day, he came home with red hair. We said, "Where did you do that?"

"My friend's house."

The next week, he came home and it was black. Again we didn't comment much. He continued to dye it different colors throughout high school. Once, someone at church asked us if Andy had quit coming to church; the man hadn't seen him in awhile! We informed him that Andy had been there all along; he was experimenting in different looks. We didn't choose to battle over his choice of hair color. Hair could be changed, and skin decorations could not.

There were other battles that normal parents probably go through; Ben wanted two cars, one to drive and one to work on. While Ed wanted to say yes for the same reason I almost said yes to Andy piercing his ear, he said no. It was already a problem to park at our house, and adding one more car—and the extra insurance cost—made it impossible. Ben wanted more animals. We said no. But the year before he married Sara, he brought home a kitten and hid it in his room. I soon discovered the black and white fur ball and couldn't make him take the kitty back to Sara's grandmother's farm. Sometimes kittens have more power than children.

As all the boys grew older, they challenged us with wanting to sleep in on Sunday morning because they had been out too late the night before. They didn't win that battle either. While they were in high school, they came to church—even if they were sleeping in the pew.

What I didn't realize as we were going through these trying times is that all of my friends who had teenagers were going through their own battle zones. It would have been nice to share some of these burdens with one another.

"God is our refuge and strength, a very present help in trouble."
(Psalm 46:1)

Most parents find themselves in all manner of battle zones with children as they grow to adulthood. Some children push hardest to assert their individuality and autonomy during the terrible twos. For others, the junior high years are full of trial, while many parents find high school is the time that fatigues their parental muscles most. In my household, the extreme emotions and bids for independence peaked during grades five and six. I thought I was safe until junior high, so the middle school tug-of-war took me by surprise.

My work as a therapist in subsequent years has enabled me to observe that same trend in many other families. I have developed my own hypothesis but have not yet read supporting research or scientific study (if offered a sizable grant, I would be happy to conduct the research!): children are maturing and developing physically earlier and earlier. Hormones are beginning to rage in many children by ages ten and eleven, and they are prepubescent. Emotional maturation, however, is lagging behind. They are exposed to so much information in the media that pushes the envelope where appropriateness is concerned, be it age inappropriate or just plain socially inappropriate. Models of surly, sarcastic, disrespectful behavior toward others, especially adults, abound on TV, in videos, and music. Kids are confused, and so are their parents. In a nutshell, puberty is starting early. Fifth grade is the new seventh grade.

Bids for marks of individuality—like piercing and body art, including tattoos, plugs, earlets, and tunnels—are becoming more and more common these days.

PLUGS, EARLETS, AND TUNNELS?

Plugs, earlets, and tunnels are usually worn in lobe piercing but can be worn in other places, like septums and cartilage. Noses, eyelids, tongues, and private parts are adorned with body jewelry. Marty's editorial: UGH!

Years ago, when Diana and Andy were playing tug-of-war, Andy would have been a trendsetter had he been permitted to pierce his ear at age nine. Kids continue to seek identity markers that push the envelope and set them apart from their parents. Diana nailed it when she wrote that she wanted to be the cool parent, and she longed for Andy's love and acceptance. She so longed for his affection that she was tempted to say yes to his request.

Sanity prevailed. The tension Diana experienced balancing her longing for Andy's love with the facts surrounding his request, family rules to date, and her duty as his mother, is parallel to tension experienced in most blended family homes.

The Internet Battle

Diana and Ed faced an all too common battle. Ben had discovered Internet pornography. This is no surprise. Internet pornographers are known for their sophisticated use of the online information delivery systems and savvy marketing. Just as the secular mental health field is discussing removal of pornography from those items designated as addictive in the Diagnostic and Statistical Manual (DSM), Christians working in the field recognize pornography use as epidemic. Parents are to be cautioned regarding the staggering use of Internet pornography by people of all ages. Children are exposed at early ages to damaging content delivered right to their homes.

Many parents find themselves in a tug-of-war regarding social networking. Social networking is not just for high school and college students anymore. The attraction of social networking sites like Facebook, MySpace, and Twitter is very strong and appeals to people of all ages, including elementary and middle school children. Those who set up social networking pages can communicate with "friends" far and near, play Internet games, and share video and audio files. Parents need to be informed consumers regarding social networking. The diverse sites offer privacy options, some with more layers of protection than others. Learn how to navigate and implement privacy settings and teach your children to do likewise.

Child advocacy specialists discourage posting pictures of minor children or even your neighborhood on networking sites. It is easy for a predator to learn information from social networking sites that may put your child at risk. In fact, I have frequently advised against sending *anything* in an e-mail or posting *anything* to a social networking site that you do not want the whole world to know. The Internet is a very public arena. Many individuals experience a false sense of privacy when online, and are tempted to engage in behaviors they might not consider in face-to-face communication. Internet bullying has had tragic consequences. Posting provocative photos has caused shame and damaged reputations.

To avoid this exposure to negative information and images:

- Do not give out personal information online—not your last name, your address, or the name of your school.

- Parents should have access to all Web site passwords.

- Monitor the amount of time your child spends online. Time limits should be different depending on age of your child or children.

- Regularly review the sites visited by family members.

- Regularly review changes to social networking sites.

- Consider implementing parental controls.

- House the computer in a common area of your home like the family room.

- Do not place a computer in your child's bedroom.

Loving parents set limits. These limits, or boundaries, protect our children. We may set limits regarding the distance our sons and daughters travel on their bikes, the types and quantity of food eaten, and the amount of time spent parked in front of video games or computers. We limit the use of phones, iPods, types of music, and other media our children view and hear. Setting limits is the mark of a loving parent but is also hard work.

One of the difficulties for a stepparent is that a child normally responds more positively to limit-setting when a relationship has been established between the child and the limit-setting adult. Most experts suggest that during the period when relationships are developing between stepparent and stepchild, the biological parent shoulder the burden of limit-setting for his or her children.

This is easier said than done when the stepparent is with the children more of the time or is the one to whom the child expresses the request for piercings and tattoos. Parents want to strike a supportive balance and make clear that each has the other's back. Unity of purpose is critical, even if one parent is more active in limit-setting than the other.

Kids will naturally push limits, frequently doing as Andy did, and raise the "But Dad would let me" charge. It seems in this case, the charge was raised as a direct challenge to Andy's stepmom.

Challenges like Andy's may make parents and stepparents forget just what battle they are fighting, or they may prepare for a fight when they might have otherwise not chosen this particular battle had the child not become oppositional.

Take a breath, and give yourself a parental "time out" if you feel that you are ready to fight over an issue that is insignificant. After you have calmed down, you may determine that setting a limit is appropriate. It may be a boundary restricting a child from a certain activity or a limit intended to teach the child that, no matter the circumstance, we are to deal respectfully with one another. The respect piece is a two-way street. Parents set the tone of respect in the home by how they honor God, honor their spouse, and deal with their children.

A note of warning: contrary behavior may be a sign of depression. A parent's remarriage and the blending into a new family may be the thing that dashes a child's hopes for reconciliation between his or her biological parents. Or it may be the point at which a child is faced with the reality of the finality of death and earthly loss. Be sensitive and alert to the warning signs of depression.

Warning Signs of Childhood Depression

- Sadness, tearfulness
- Loss of pleasure or interest in activities that had previously been enjoyable
- Difficulty concentrating
- Helplessness, hopelessness
- Guilt
- Isolation
- Suicidal talk, focus on death

- Change in appetite, either greater appetite or less

- Sleep disturbance

- Agitation

- Lethargy

- Clinging

- Self-harm behaviors

Depressed children typically will not exhibit all of the above symptoms. If you suspect your child is experiencing depression, check in with your pediatrician, family physician, counselor, or a child psychologist. When a child speaks of suicide or self-harm, always err on the side of caution. Safeguarding our children is definitely a battle worth fighting.

FOR MORE ON ~ PARENTING

Allender, Dan B. *How Children Raise Parents*. Colorado Springs, 2003.

Cloud, Henry, and John Townsend. *Raising Great Kids: Parenting with Grace and Truth*. Grand Rapids: Zondervan, 1999).

Clark, Chap, and Dee Clark. *Disconnected: Parenting Teens in a MySpace World*. Grand Rapids: Baker Books, 2007.

Clark, Chap, and Steve Rabey. *When Kids Hurt: Help for Adults Navigating the Adolescent Maze*. Grand Rapids: Baker Books, 2009.

Gottman, John, and Joan Declaire. *Raising an Emotionally Intelligent Child: The Heart of Parenting*. New York: Fireside, 1997.

Hart, Dr. Archibald, and Dr. Catherine Hart Weber. *Stressed or Depressed: A Practical and Inspirational Guide for Parents of Hurting Teens*. Brentwood, TN: Integrity Publishers, 2005.

"For we are His workmanship." (Ephesians 2:10)

22

Whose Money Is It?

Money. That a five-letter word can cause so much angst in a home; maybe it should never be said aloud. There never seems to be enough of it, or someone spends more than he or she should, or someone wants to save instead of spend. In a normal marriage, those issues can cause days of not speaking to each other. In a blended marriage, it can be disastrous.

Our family, being blended because of death and remarriage, brought some interesting challenges. There wasn't any child support or alimony that needed to be paid. Instead, we had to figure out what to do with unequal social security payments, life insurance, the money from selling my home, and tithing. That's a lot of numbers to toss around. I don't do numbers—just can't. In fact, I call a friend from a dressing room to figure out how much something costs when it's on the 75 percent off rack. If you want to see and hear drama in our house, just ask me to balance the checkbook. It gets ugly. There are tears, and I toss pens across the room as my frustration rises.

Then there is Ed. Numbers love him. They line up in their tight little formations and add and subtract themselves like fine-tuned dancers. The two of us communicating about finances becomes a very fast two-step: he tries to explain, and I take two steps away. Somehow he has managed to keep things running without my help. I think he should continue—forever.

We were out on a Friday night date at our favorite pie place. "What do you want to do about the money we have from Debbi and John?" Ed asked.

"Spend it." I visualized gleaming wood floors, a screened-in porch, new furniture, and shoes—glorious shoes! Andy would go for that; he loved shopping for shoes.

Ed shook his head, not a good sign. "We can't spend it on stuff. What I'm asking is would you like to keep your money from John separate, keep my name off the account?"

After John died, Uncle Jack was my financial person. He had known Ed a long time and had a great respect for him, yet he had suggested keeping our accounts separate for at least a year. I didn't like that idea. I think if you love someone enough to marry and let him be involved in your children's lives, you should share the expenses. "No. I want your name on everything."

"Are you sure?"

"Are you planning on leaving me and taking all the money? If you do, I get the kids." I can count to three.

"No. I agree with you. I think we should combine it all. That way, you'll be able to stay at home with the boys instead of work."

Did he say "instead of work"? My schedule for the week with all its little colored boxes of tasks grew large in my mind. Blue for activities, red for appointments, green for chores, yellow for menus; I even had to switch to squares and circles for some things since there weren't enough different colored markers! I took a breath, let it out slowly, then said, "I work. Taking care of kids and a house is not easy. The laundry for five people is going to take a lot of time."

"That's not what I meant. Focus. I know money isn't your favorite topic. We need to figure out income, expenses, titles to the houses and cars."

He wrote down numbers on paper and flipped it around for me to read. "Just let me know when I need to sign papers, okay?" I said. "It's date night, not a math class."

Ed did as I asked. All of the cars and the houses were legally put in both of our names. We had learned from experience that not having the word *or* in a title can cause serious problems when a spouse dies. You have to get death certificates to sell anything. Ed set aside money to do repairs on the home in Missouri to be able to sell it, doing the labor himself and saving us money. At first we thought we would rent out the house and someday retire there. Then after the first batch of renters left, we knew we lived too far away to be caretakers. So we sold it when the market wasn't at its best and barely broke even.

It became clear that both of our perspectives on money were needed. I was the emotional one in the relationship, and as soon as Ed said that money was tight, I was ready to cancel vacations, dinners out, and all activities. Ed would reassure me that we weren't being tossed out on the street and would find a way for money to be available for the extras by picking up an extra job or two. I would cut back on the amount of meals we would eat out and clip more coupons.

There were separate accounts for college educations, and we put them all in one, hoping to get a better interest rate. Then September 11, 2001 happened, and like many Americans, we lost a great deal of our money. Instead of us being able to pay for the boys' education completely, they had to take out loans. That would have occurred even if we hadn't combined the accounts.

The amount of the social security checks for the care of Ben and Josh was more than Andy's. We combined those as well, and the money went to food, clothes, and paying for the boys' activities.

Ben and Andy were entering junior high, and we felt it was time to teach them about money. I had read something about assigning a monetary value to each chore. At the end of the week, the chores that were done were paid for, and those that were not completed were not paid for. That money went to Mom, who would have to do the chore they didn't do. It was a long list and included doing their laundry. We also gave them the option of buying their lunches or taking them. If they took them, they could keep the money we allotted for bought lunches. The plan also required they put 10 percent into savings and 10 percent into either the church offering or a parentally approved charity. Most of the time the plan worked well. Sometimes they needed extra money for an unexpected expense, and as parents, we helped. We were proud of the choices they made in their giving. Now as adults, they are capable of budgeting their money. I am proud of them. They learned something as children that I did not.

There are days I still say, "Hey, where did all the money go? I thought we had more than this. And how much do we have now?"

Once again, Ed will bring out paper and pen and line up those perfect numbers with printed titles next to them and attempt to explain it. My brain gets fuzzy; my palms sweat. I start thinking of cute shoes, and then I suggest we go for ice cream. He agrees every time.

We both agree that the money issue is a major emotional hurdle. It's as big as learning how to discipline each other's children or adopting them. Money was never discussed with the boys. They didn't know about the social security checks or the money from the life insurance policies. As a couple, we decided it wasn't something children needed to know or to worry about.

Sometimes Andy would question Ed about who the house belonged to since he and Ed had been living here before we came. Ed always answered that the house belonged to everyone. There were times when Andy would suggest Ed should make all the rules because he was the one bringing in the money. That didn't resonate well with either of his parents. Now that he's grown, he understands that, though I was paid in kisses and hugs instead of money, I worked hard.

> *"Do not be anxious about anything, but in everything by prayer and supplication with thanksgiving let your requests be made known to God." (Philippians 4:6)*

Money tops the list of frequent sources of marital conflict. People fight over money. Blended families face many complex money issues: child support, inheritances, combining assets or not, managing debt, and on and on. How do blended couples avoid the money fights?

Diana and Ed had detailed discussions about the assets each brought to the marriage. It is important to discuss this information, as well as any level of indebtedness. Before you start studying the facts and figures, have frank discussions regarding your attitudes about money. How similarly or differently do you and your spouse deal with financial matters? Together answer the following questions:

- How did your families of origin handle money?
- Were you aware of financial concerns in your parents' household?
- Did you learn to save?
- How did you handle money in your prior marriage?
- Do you consider yourself a saver or a spender?
- Will both spouses work?
- Should children receive allowances?
- If so, is the allowance earned for completion of chores or not?
- How many credit cards do you, or should you, carry?
- Do you use a debit card?
- Will one or both of you carry a debit card?
- Will it be for a shared account or two different accounts?
- What will be the process for tracking debits?

- Do you charge items regularly?
- If so, do you pay off balances monthly?
- Do you work from a budget?
- Are you a good steward?

After you have discussed these items and other aspects of money management, you will determine how, as a couple, you will deal with financial concerns. You need to address whether you will have separate bank accounts and checkbooks for the two of you. If you determine that you will have one checking account, then you must select the primary carrier of the checkbook. Will that person be responsible for balancing your accounts? If you are using debit cards, you must have a means to track your separate expenditures.

TERRY

"At different times, we were both supposed to receive child support but didn't, and then we also both paid child support to our former spouses. Noel and I didn't see our money as his and mine. We saw our responsibilities and then did our best to make things happen properly."

SYLVIA

"All earnings and benefits went into one pot to pay for the house, utilities, food, etc. Even so, we lived from paycheck to paycheck. It soon became apparent that I had to pay the bills in order to get them paid on time."

Spouses receiving or paying child support often experience further complications. Some of those complications are financial, and some are relational. Maintaining cordial, respectful relations with former spouses is highly advisable: you may need to compromise with them in the coming years. My father used to introduce people to my husband's parents with, "This is Vern and Marie. We share grandchildren." You remain connected to your ex because you share children. Cordial behavior toward them will make discussions of tough subjects, like money, a little easier.

If one or both of you enter your marriage with assets, will you keep them separate for yourself and your children? If this is your intent, check with a lawyer regarding the laws pertaining to separate or commingled property. Many blended families establish a joint household account for family expenses but keep other accounts separate. Other couples, like Ed and Diana, combine everything. Still others will combine the spouses' assets but retain the children's accounts separately.

Review wills, guardianship provisions, and beneficiaries on life insurance and retirement policies. Make sure your spouse is informed regarding these things. A recent widow at our church was surprised to learn when the will was read that her late husband had named a niece as his life insurance beneficiary. Ann was perplexed and troubled by this news, and her bereavement was intensified. The death of Ann's husband was unexpected, and the stipulations in his insurance policy may have merely been an oversight or something on his list of "things I need to do" but never did, and not a deliberate act intended to exclude Ann. Those who knew Joe think that it probably was just an oversight, but the pain that it caused was great nonetheless.

So get your financial house in order. Review assets and debts, spell out clearly each spouse's financial obligations, and determine who pays what. Perhaps, like Diana, numbers and accounting overwhelm you. We know that money is often a source of friction between spouses and a sensitive, complex issue for the blended family. Consulting early on with an accountant or financial planner who specializes in the blended family dynamic may be a wise investment. Careful financial planning is a part of wise stewardship. And as you attend to the tedious job of organizing your finances, remember your blessings. God is good.

"I will sing of the steadfast love of the Lord, forever."
(Psalm 89:1)

23

Happy Holidays
Meets Strategic Planning

We had just finished our first ever Thanksgiving meal as a blended family at Ed's parents' home. They had invited my mom, helping make the transition to a different kind of holiday easier for me. The talk turned to Christmas, and I announced I had all of the shopping done. There was a moment of silence as the new relatives looked at me in shock.

"You don't shop the day after Thanksgiving?" Ed's sister asked.

"I like to be done early because the crowds bother me."

"Well, just remember the day after Christmas is my house." Ed's mom said.

"Christmas Eve is my house," my mom added.

"Good, that will leave us Christmas Day for our family."

"Nope, we have Aunt Shirley's that day," said Ed.

When would we fit in John's parents and Andy's grandmother's Christmas? The days of December were filling up fast. There weren't that many weekends.

The first year was not fun. We spent so much time traveling that everyone was worn out. There was barely time to remember we were celebrating Christ's arrival. The second year, I tried to plan better, asking John's parents if we could do Christmas earlier, and we asked the same question of Andy's grandmother. And then there was the Sunday School program to work around. Every weekend in December became about getting gifts.

December is a month fraught with emotions for Ed and me. Putting up the tree meant seeing ornaments John and I had made together our first year of marriage. Special ornaments Debbi had picked out for Ed and Andy would be in the boxes too. Even though we didn't hang those ornaments, we wanted them available if one of the boys chose to hang one.

Debbi died December 23, making it difficult for Ed to enjoy the season. Andy seemed to be more argumentative during the month as well. When it came time to set up the Christmas tree, he would be excited, and then his mood would change to surly and disrespectful. There was one Christmas that Ed found me upstairs on the floor begging God to let Andy enjoy just one Christmas, so the rest of us could too. No matter how much planning, baking, and decorating I did, it seemed I could not get Christmas to be a happy occasion for Ed. Both of us went through the motions, and I don't think the boys noticed our quietness.

John's parents were from Belgium, and they celebrated St. Nicholas Day (December 6). I wanted to continue that tradition. So on St. Nick's, the boys would check their stockings and find a new ornament and a piece for their nativity scene. I wanted them to have a nice one to take with them when they moved out and started a family of their own.

I made Advent wreaths for each of them to help count down the days until Christ was born. They each had a tree in their room and lights they could hang. Josh stretched lights across his room, and it's possible it was as bright as the star of Bethlehem.

We started changing things in an attempt to take the focus off of getting gifts. Along with John's mom and dad and my sister-in-law and brother-in-law, we decided to adopt a local family through my sister-in-law's school. We split the wish list between our families, and then we met at the Lesire home two weeks before Christmas. John's mom would make a Christmas dinner for us, and for dessert she would bring out the traditional Buche de Noel (a divine flourless chocolate cake rolled with chocolate whipped cream, symbolizing a Yule log). After it was devoured and the kitchen cleaned, everyone gathered on the floor. We would snip wrapping paper and bows and stick them on gifts, and sometimes bows ended up on someone's head. We all had more fun than if we had sat on the couches opening gifts for ourselves.

On Christmas Eve, we would go to my mom's for brunch and play board games. We stopped going to Ed's aunt's house, and for a few years, we went to Andy's grandmother's home during the week. Christmas morning would be for our family. On that evening, we would prepare a meal for grandparents and good friends. That tradition continues, and it is the only holiday when relatives come to our home. As the years went by, I leaned on my faith for comfort, focusing on why this holiday is so important. I would never have the picture-perfect Christmas when breakfast doesn't catch on fire in the oven, and I would never have the family photo in which everyone is smiling. Christmas is not about the gifts or even family. It's about my Savior coming here to save me. That's what makes Christmas perfect.

Our holidays are set for now. For Easter, we go to Ed's parents' home. When the kids were little, they would have an Easter egg hunt. Now it's just Ed's mom, and she still wants to have Easter at her house. We love going there, stuffing ourselves, and then taking the annual Easter walk after dinner.

Fourth of July is my mom's holiday. We pile into our cars and drive across the river, purchase way too many sparklers and rockets, and then drive some more to get to her home. My stepdad makes the best barbecued hamburgers, the women play scrabble, and then at dusk the men shoot fireworks off over the pond.

"God has called you to peace." (1 Corinthians 7:15)

HOLIDAY HAVOC

Do you find yourself dreading the approaching holidays and longing for them to be behind you? Coordinating holiday celebrations can be one of the more frustrating aspects of blending families. Maintain a calm spirit as you hear the holiday refrain—perhaps as often as the carols pipe through the sound system at the mall—"This is how we've always done it!" Remaining calm will help you bravely consider plausible alternatives to situations in which the pieces just don't seem to fit.

Diana bravely negotiated with the many families to whom she and her family were related, and whom they loved, so that they were included in important celebrations. Sometimes this meant creating a new calendar or process for holiday observations.

Do you and your family make the rounds on big holidays, like Christmas, Thanksgiving, and Easter? Or do you alternate, celebrating Thanksgiving with one set of family members and Christmas with the other, then swap things up the next season? Making the rounds gives the sense that we are staying connected to and honoring family members, but it may be exhausting—particularly if you are loading overtired children in and out of car seats, missing naps, and hauling the same sleepy kids out after a fifteen-minute snooze en route to Grandma Sally's house.

Small children are not equipped to function well and happily when sleep deprived and over-stimulated by sugar and excitement—a scary combination. Look to simplify your celebrations as much as possible. Consider your children's developmental stages and normal daily routine when organizing holiday visits. Simplifying your holiday celebrations may be especially helpful for parents of small children.

Seek Peace

When multiple sets of parents are involved, adult cooperation is imperative. This is necessary not only for the benefit of small children, but for big ones too. You may have actually established some of your holiday practices due to court or divorce stipulations. Seek peace, again, for the benefit of your children and the benefit of your own health.

Survey respondent and stepmom Louise wrote that she spent every Christmas with her husband's ex-wife because that's where the children would be. Louise did not want to deprive her husband of a Christmas or Easter spent with his children. She did this for decades, until her husband passed away. This kind of accommodation is not possible for many blended families. But you can seek peace as you transfer children from one home to the next.

Keep in mind that creating holiday memories that a family will treasure is likely as important for your former spouse as it is for you. Singing around the Christmas tree, candlelight Advent services, and Sunday School Christmas programs create lasting memories. Equally strong are the memories of holiday fights and conflict.

More Holiday Havoc

Are your holidays always spent at the same home, and it is never yours? Introduce the idea of rotating which home will host the celebration. If you have always celebrated at Grandma's farm, there may be resistance at first. But more often than not, even Grandma will appreciate taking turns hosting celebrations.

Survey respondent Terry wrote that on Thanksgiving, she and her husband, Noel, cooked and invited all the kids, grandkids, and extended family to dinner. They allowed children to invite whom they wanted, regardless. So they often had grandparents, uncles, cousins, in-laws, step- and half-relatives, girlfriends, and boyfriends. They even welcomed other parents.

After supper, the couple would instruct those who wanted to participate in their Christmas gift exchange to put their names into the bowl. Then the bowl was passed, and each participant would choose one name. The only rule was that you could not select your own spouse. Then the names were recorded and posted on Terry's refrigerator door, where they stayed until Christmas Day, when the family would return for an afternoon potluck meal and gift exchange.

Terry's process allowed everyone to have Christmas with their natal families in the morning and then gather together at Terry's later in the day. The family would sit in a circle eating and visiting and open gifts one at a time to see what each person received. Terry reports that gifts were well thought out and often homemade.

Some families hold celebrations and reunions at a neutral location. This may be due to space needs rather than family conflict. Perhaps your family's celebration would be more enjoyable if held in the church basement, a banquet center, or the pavilion of a local park.

If rotating locations is not an option, suggest family members provide more assistance with food items, help with the setup, and help clean up when the function is over. Perhaps a schedule of duties that rotates year to year will help ensure that one person or family doesn't get stuck with all the tedious jobs or expense, unless they want this. An easy way to keep track is to divide by household: "Terry and Noel's family is responsible for setup this year, Mary and Dave for cleanup, and everyone brings a dish to share. Next year we swap." Or take a tip from Ed and assign duties by even or odd years.

Among the more complicated holidays for blended families to negotiate are Mother's Day and Father's Day. These are often emotionally charged holidays, due to expectations and family history. Families that have blended post-divorce may have sensitive spots where the stepparent is concerned. If custody arrangements preclude your child from being with her mom on Mother's Day, take the high road. Do not hinder your son or daughter from phoning her mom or sending a card. And vice versa. Children love both their parents.

Often stepmoms and dads feel left out of Mother's and Father's Day observances. Families that have experienced the death of one parent and subsequently blended with another may find Mother's or Father's Day triggers a fresh flood of grief. This is normal and doesn't mean the individual doesn't love and care for the stepparent. If you have shared parenting duties with a spouse who is not the biological parent to your child, acknowledge the important role they have played in your family. Encourage their stepchildren to do the same.

Ed's first wife died two days before Christmas. The loss of a spouse, parent, or other loved one that occurs on or near a holiday changes the tone of that holiday. Be sensitive to the fact that your spouse or stepchild may have a very tender heart during holidays that mark a significant loss. The depth of pain may change over time, but check in with those family members regarding acceptable—tolerable—holiday practices. You may choose not to bake Debbi's favorite cookie because your husband and son can't bear the smell. Or your Andy might want the recipe and honor his late mom by baking and decorating those cookies himself. If in doubt, ask. Gently.

LARRY

Survey respondent Larry said that he felt uncertain about including adult children in blended family celebrations. Larry and Doris married late in life, following the deaths of their spouses. Both had grown kids and grandkids. After the wedding, most holidays were "his" or "hers." His kids came on one day; hers came on another—different celebrations with the family members from their first marriages. The result was that the extended family remained at arm's length from one another.

Larry's son, Craig, said he would have liked getting to know Doris's family more and wouldn't have minded sharing some holidays. The distance between families was finally broken when Larry was hospitalized, and Doris's children came to the hospital to visit him. There Craig was able to sit and talk with his stepsiblings and finally get to know them a little better. Craig said he wished it had happened sooner.

You don't need to wait until someone is ill to bring adult children together. Planning a combined family event on a holiday other than Christmas—when no gifts are exchanged—may be a place to start. Families are less stressed during lower-key celebrations, like a Fourth of July barbecue or Memorial Day picnic. If you are unsure whether shared holidays or family functions are of interest, just ask. If they say no, continue as you have in the past. But you might be surprised.

Focusing on the real reason for the celebration can help families resolve details about how to observe that holiday. Christmas and Easter are celebrations of the gifts we have been given through Christ our Lord. During Advent, the weeks prior to Christmas, devotions around the Advent wreath and Christmas caroling can bring our focus back from commercial concerns to the good news of our Savior's birth. Spending part of your holiday season preparing gift baskets for the needy, participating in a winter coat drive for the underprivileged, or serving in a soup kitchen can remind families of the needs of others and be reminders of the blessings they enjoy. And remember that other families feel the same stresses you're feeling with your family obligations. You are not alone.

> "The LORD your God is in your midst,
> a mighty One who will save;
> He will rejoice over you with gladness;
> He will quiet you by His love;
> He will exult over you with loud singing."
> (Zephaniah 3:17)

24

Fleeing Birds,
Empty Rooms, and Loving
the One You're With

Our home was eerily clean. There were no empty glasses strewn throughout the house with dried juice cemented to the bottom. The bathroom towel stayed on the towel bar instead of lying on the counter. And the quiet! Oh my! Even the washer and dryer had stilled their daily rumble.

All our boys had turned into men, and they each left home in a different way. Ben, our planner, was first, eager to be an adult and on his own. He married his high school sweetheart right after college. Andy, our rebel, took off next, choosing to live in a small house with five other boys, where he could be free of parental restrictions. Josh, the baby, was the last to go and the first to travel so far from home. He went to Concordia University Chicago with the intention of becoming a pastor, but then he changed his mind and went into business, got engaged, and remained in Chicago.

It all happened so fast. They all left in the same year. There are five years between the older two and Josh, which should have given us more time to have him at home. That left me and Ed alone—for the first time ever.

I sat across the table from Ed at dinner. I had made an "as close as I can get" gourmet meal just for the two of us. He spread the paper across his side of the table, started to read, and never looked up at me the entire meal. I know because I stared at him, waiting for the conversation. You know the conversation? The one you think you'll be having when the kids finally leave the house. All during the time that you weren't able to speak to each other in full sentences without using your secret decoder ring, you imagine the days when you can sit with your spouse and share those deep thoughts over a good meal?

It wasn't happening.

Something had to be done. We needed to claim this time before we had grandchildren or one of the boys moved back.

"Do you think any of the boys will move back home?" For a moment, that sounded like an answer. "Maybe Andy could live with us while he finishes his master's?"

"I was thinking we should turn Josh's room into a closet. We could break through the back wall in my closet and take out the door to his room. We would have a master suite then, especially if we enlarged the bathroom. We can keep Andy's room for a guestroom, and you already made Ben's room into a sewing room. So there wouldn't be room for them to come back. Besides, you don't really want that for them, do you?"

"Maybe." A closet out of Josh's room? That would be huge. I liked that idea, but I wasn't ready to eliminate their rooms. Not yet.

We had already rehabbed a house together to pay for Josh's tuition, and after falling through the floor, I wasn't ready to go back to bonding that way. On our Friday date nights, we had taken swing and country dance lessons.

"Maybe we should take ballroom dancing?"

"No. I'm not doing that," Ed said. "Let's do something else, like ride the entire Katy Trail on our bikes."

"I don't think so. It's too far for me. Let's take a class on photography."

"No, don't like that idea either."

This wasn't going well. So far we had settled into the routine of me watching Ed read the paper at dinner, and in the evening, I got to watch over 150 channels on television fly by in an hour as Ed rapidly switched them.

"I guess we aren't compatible. How did I not see that before I married you, Ed?"

"What?" The volume lessened on the television. "We're compatible. We do things together all the time."

Aha! I had his attention. "Like what?"

"We like traveling and eating out. We're always looking for new restaurants with a gluten-free menu for you. That's been an adventure. We ride bikes together on the weekends. And on Sundays, we drive around looking at open houses; you like to do that."

"True, but shouldn't there be more? Look at the people in the commercials; they're taking cruises and sitting on the beach watching sunsets, not hockey."

"That's not real life. Besides, we're both still working. I'm going to be laying bricks forever, and you're writing. Don't worry about it; we'll find things to do."

I continued to think about what we could do, what we could afford, which wasn't a lot since we hadn't recovered financially from September 11. I thought about what I was willing to do. I'm not a big adventure advocate. I actually like being home 98 percent of the time. I think I was hoping Ed would come up with some great ideas and drag me along. I talked to my friends who were going through the same phase of life, and they were just as clueless, even though they weren't in blended marriages.

"Maybe we're too comfortable, Ed. We don't have anything to stand for or against. Our entire marriage, it's been us against the boys. We don't have anything new to say to each other."

"So let's get out of the comfort zone."

"Can we get a puppy?"

"I was thinking we could do the service project this summer with the church."

Wait a minute; I didn't want to go in this direction! I wanted time together, not with an entire community. "I don't think I'm Camp Pioneer material."

"It'll be fun. We'll be in the car together for fifteen hours both ways, lots of time to talk and discuss what to do in the future. Lake Erie is there, and you like lakes."

"But this is so different. We can't just take off and explore the area. We're expected to work while we're there, and," I pulled out my trump card, "it costs a lot of money."

"I'll make it work. Besides, think of the stories we'll have to tell. You'll get to see Niagara Falls. Plus it will give us a feel for how it would be to work with Laborers for Christ." I scrunched my nose. "That's your dream, not mine. I want to take ballroom dance lessons."

We went to camp. Sometimes you have to give new things a try. Ed had a wonderful time at camp interacting with people from our church. I did not. I was sick for the first part of the week, and I had recently been told not to eat gluten. So I prepared and ate all of my meals in the cabin. Alone. I went to the beach once. During the day, I helped organize the craft shed and after devotions, went back to our cabin and slept. If I had felt better, the experience would have been different.

However, we did something we had never done together, or with our first spouses, or with our children. We had made a new memory, complete with new stories to tell.

On the way home, we discussed our future plans and concluded that we're doing okay together. Even though we hadn't had a child together, all of the boys felt like mine. I may not have experienced Andy in the womb and the labor pains, but through the years, I learned that wasn't what was important. Having Andy as my third child was my request fulfilled by God.

Through the years, our date nights incorporated activities we might have done before we had children, allowing us to know each other. We've attended conferences in other states and explored the surrounding cities—even checking out the Nashville Public Library, one of the original Carnegie Libraries. While we might not ever be able to cruise the oceans or walk the streets of Paris, there is an abundance of inexpensive things for us to do in our own cities. We attend art fairs, chili cook-offs, and the Taste of St. Louis. There are free concerts in the local park. Someday we hope to vacation with our children and grandchildren.

Then again, I'm still holding out for ballroom dance lessons. Maybe next year? And about that huge closet? I think I'm ready for it.

> *"Where you go I will go, and where you lodge I will lodge. Your people shall be my people, and your God my God." (Ruth 1:16)*

All of a sudden, it seemed, Ed and Diana's boys had become men. Like many couples who have shared the blended family experience, when the boys moved out, Ed and Diana were alone together for the very first time. They had looked forward to finally experiencing life as a couple and began in earnest to redefine who they were as husband and wife.

They would always be mother and father to three incredible men and mother- and father-in-law to their precious daughters-in-law. That wouldn't change. And though the nest was empty, with the addition of their daughters-in-law, the blending process continued. But so many other things were different. It was quiet.

The fact that all the boys left in rapid succession was a bit of a surprise, but Diana and Ed navigated this transition better than some. They had always enjoyed bike riding and now could do that more. Home renovation projects created an environment that encouraged solo and couple pursuits, including the addition of Diana's sewing room and a remodeled home office. From his reclaimed garage workshop, Ed built a bike rack for four, enabling the couple to travel to new places and bike. Sometimes they take off alone; other times Ed loads the rack, and they travel with friends to try a new path, see a new sight.

Long before they grew to men, it was clear that Andy, Ben, and Josh shared their dad's sense of adventure. As they ride off on their bikes, Diana ringing her bell to alert pedestrians, I wonder if that sense of adventure has infected her too. Their empty nest is a pretty happy place.

Not so for some couples.

EMPTY NEST MARRIAGES

The empty nest is frequently a period of insecurity. But with change comes the opportunity for growth.

Challenges	Opportunities
Identity loss	Redefining identity
Loneliness	Time for individual interests
Insecure period	Greater flexibility
Feeling you no longer know your spouse	More time to nurture marriage

We each respond to change in different ways. Many parents experience a deep sadness caused by their fleeing birds. If this is true in your case, consider the following:

- See your doctor.
- Take a vacation.
- Exercise.
- Spend time with your spouse.
- Keep in touch with friends, relatives, and those birds who have flown.
- Try something new.
- Increase devotional time.
- Give yourself grace. God has.

"Even to your old age I am He, and to gray hairs I will carry you. I have made, and I will bear; I will carry and will save." (Isaiah 46:4)

MY STORY OF OUR
SLOWLY EMPTYING NEST

I remember the day we brought our firstborn home from the hospital. We had prepared diligently for parenthood. Even before I became pregnant, I thought my experience as a much older sister, a very busy teenage babysitter, and aunt had given me some pretty good skills. During my pregnancy, I devoured books on the subject, on labor and delivery, and on parenting. My husband and I attended ten weeks of Lamaze classes (ten weeks!), studied high chairs, strollers, and any manner of infant paraphernalia.

On the trip home from the hospital, our son Erik fell asleep in his jumbo deluxe car seat. We didn't want to wake him by lifting him out of the seat, so Vern unstrapped the car seat and carried it up a long flight of stairs to our apartment. (This was before the pumpkin seats that pop in and out of the car easily.) Erik's was a monster car seat—big, heavy, and very safe. Vern set the car seat down on the floor. The baby was still sleeping, so my husband and I settled down on the couch facing him. We looked at our son. We looked at each other. We had read all the books, gone to classes. But he was ours now, and we didn't know what to do. Then he woke up.

Preparing for the empty nest is a little like preparing to fill the nest. During your son or daughter's senior year of high school, you visit colleges, collect catalogues, shop for extra-long fitted sheets, and mentally remodel your home. For most of us, the preparations to bring a child into our home are exciting.

But many parents are surprised at how difficult the preparation for high school graduation, college, or your child's marriage can be. I became a different person during my firstborn's senior year. I cried a lot, and I am not a crier. Erik investigated colleges on either coast, and I got lonely. It was September, and he wouldn't graduate until May, but I missed him already. And he was looking at universities that violated my requirement that the school chosen must be within a day's drive of home. If his appendix burst, I would need to get there quickly; he would need me.

I couldn't believe the pendulum of emotions and how easily I was brought to tears, which I hid behind closed doors. No one told me that your child's senior year could be so painful. Then they leave, and for a little while, you don't know what to do. You look at your spouse and figure it out. He reads the paper, or maybe you do. You take ballroom dance lessons or ride the Katy Trail.

When my daughter Heidi left, I did better. I cried less during her senior year. When the tears did fall, I gave myself the grace I encouraged for others. Heidi and I enjoyed her college visit and the preparations for transition to dorm life. She went farther from home than her older brother, who, after all my tears, traveled only twenty-five miles from the nest.

When freshman orientation came, Heidi's dad and I hauled her belongings to Charleston, joining the queue of parents unloading mini-fridges and computers. I was proud that I didn't park myself on her bed and begin a deeply spiritual and uplifting discussion with her roommate that could have lasted until tomorrow. She didn't have to ask or beg me to leave! And I only sobbed a little on the two and a half hour drive home. Maybe by the time Travis and Kristen flee the nest, I'll have it down.

Diana has a pamphlet somewhere from the dance studio. Kristen is eleven, so that gives me time to warm Vern up to the thought of gliding across the dance floor. Maybe by the time she flies, I'll know how to tango.

> *"I pray that out of His glorious riches He may strengthen you with power through His Spirit in your inner being, so that Christ may dwell in your hearts through faith. And I*

pray that you, being rooted and established in love, may have power, together with all the saints, to grasp how wide and long and high and deep is the love of Christ, and to know this love that surpasses knowledge—that you may be filled to the measure of all the fullness of God. Now to Him who is able to do immeasurably more than all we ask or imagine, according to His power that is at work within us, to Him be glory in the church and in Christ Jesus throughout all generations, forever and ever! Amen."
(Ephesians 3:16–21)

Notes

CHAPTER 5

1. F. Dean Lueking, *Let's Talk Marriage: A Guide for Couples Preparing to Marry* (Grand Rapids: Eerdmans, 2001), 83–84.
2. Mary Fairchild, "How to Find a Church," http://christianity.about.com/od/churchandcommunity/ht/chooseachurch.htm.

CHAPTER 10

1. Jim Burns, *Creating an Intimate Marriage: Rekindle Romance Through Affection, Warmth and Encouragement* (Bloomington, MN: Bethany House, 2006), 60–64.
2. Burns, *Creating an Intimate Marriage*, 67.
3. Jim Burns, *Teaching Your Children Healthy Sexuality: A Biblical Approach to Preparing Them for Life* (Bloomington, MN: Bethany House, 2008), 38.

CHAPTER 13

1. Henry Cloud and John Townsend, *Boundaries with Kids: When to say YES, When to Say NO, to Help Your Children Gain Control of their Lives* (Grand Rapids: Zondervan, 1998), 17.
2. See Foster Cline and Jim Fay, *Parenting with Love and Logic: Teaching Children Responsibility* (Colorado Springs: Pinion Press, 1990), 13; and Cloud and Townsend, *Boundaries with Kids*, 26.

CHAPTER 14

1. Maxine Marsolini, *Blended Families: Creating Harmony as You Build a New Home Life* (Chicago: Moody Press, 2000), 111.
2. Marsolini, *Blended Families*, 112.

CHAPTER 15

1. Leanne Ely, "The Importance of the Family Dinner Table," Main Street Mom, 2001, http://mainstreetmom.com/parenting/din.htm.
2. Alan Greene, "Family Mealtime: All for One and One for All," 2009, www.drgreene.com/article/family-mealtime-all-one-and-one-all?tid=145.

CHAPTER 17

1. Greg DeNeal, *Living With the Echoes of Grief* (St. Louis: Kaleo Counseling, unpublished manuscript, 2009).